what confucius really said

what confucius really said

THE COMPLETE ANALECTS IN A SKOPOS-CENTRIC TRANSLATION

translated by

Chris Wen-chao Li

MAISON 174

San Francisco

Cover image: Meningsverschil tussen een acht-jarige jongen en Confucius (by Yashima Gakutei, c. 1829), courtesy of Rijksmuseum, Amsterdam

Publisher's Cataloging-in-Publication data

Li, Chris Wen-chao:
    What Confucius really said: The complete Analects in a
    skopos-centric translation / translated with an introduction
    by Chris Wen-chao Li.
    p. cm.

ISBN-10: 1727464494
ISBN-13: 978-1727464498

1. Philosophy—Eastern. 2. Religion—Confucianism. 3. Literary collections—Asian—Chinese. 4. Literary collections—Asian—general.
I. Li, Chris Wen-chao, 1968– II. Li, Wen-chao, 1968– III. Title.

Published by:

MAISON 174
174 Stratford Drive
San Francisco, CA 94132
United States of America

CONTENTS

Translator's Preface

The expression "lost in translation" has no better application than to the *Analects* of Confucius — a compendium of lively banter and engaging exchanges between Confucius and his contemporaries, one that touches upon culture, fashion, arts, and society, making fun of celebrities and political figures of the day with juicy quotes from bestselling books as well as popular lyrics from the most widely-circulated songs, all of which, unfortunately, is lost on the modern reader — lost in translations that, out of good scholarly intention, seek to faithfully preserve historical reference: engaging personalities are reduced a scramble of unintelligible names; the wit, the charm, the vitriol, and the humor of the Master are crushed under the weight of ancient history, little of which is familiar to or of interest to the contemporary reader.

In this version of the *Analects* we do things differently. We not only translate the language, but transpose the culture. In the world's first skopos-centered translation of the Confucian *Analects*, we remove the distractions of history and culture by teleporting Confucius into modern society and allowing him to speak in a contemporary American idiom: where he quotes from the masterworks of his day, we counter with classical passages of our own; where he sings from popular songs, we take lines from our own lyrical repertoire. Politicians of antiquity are replaced with their doppelgangers from the American political landscape; Chinese dynasties are swapped for the empires of Greece and Rome. The result is a work of equivalent effect, through which the rhetorical force and conversational style of Confucius becomes evident, allowing the ideas of Confucius the man to shine through.

Confucius the man appealed to audiences of his day precisely because he excelled at appropriating current affairs and celebrities of the moment to foreground his ideas — that is, affairs and celebrities that were current to him but not to us. Thus in the *Analects* we find a long list of historical characters, including the Duke of Zhōu, Duke Āi of Lǔ, Duke Dìng of Lǔ, Duke Jǐng of Qí, King Wén of Zhōu, and King Wǔ of Zhōu, to mention a few, whom readers without a background in Chinese history will find disorienting. Often the lay reader is forced to trawl through a sea of footnotes that attempt to explain the significance of each historical reference, in the process sacrificing the immediacy and arguably killing the joy of reading.

To illustrate, let us look at *Analects* 14.22, which, in a more traditional translation appears as:

> Chvn Chvngdz had killed Jyen-gung. Confucius bathed and went to court. He reported to Ai-gung, Chvn Hwan has killed his ruler. I ask to punish him. The Prince said, Report it to the Three Masters.[1]

But who is Chvn Chvngdz? Who is Jyen-gung? What is their relationship? And who are Ai-gung and Chvn Hwan? Why do they need to report the incident to "the Three Masters", whoever they might be? None of this can be deduced from the primary text, for which footnotes longer than the passage itself are required to fill in the background. Here we introduce a different approach gleaned from theories of translation action, in which the translator's aim is to craft a *translatum* — an offer of information in the target language that imitates the

---

[1] From Brooks, E. Bruce, and A. Taeko Brooks. 1998. *The Original Analects: Sayings of Confucius and His Successors*, p.123. New York: Columbia University Press.

information proffered in the source language[2]. In this case, rather than turn the *Analects* into a grueling lesson in history, we instead switch out the unfamiliar characters for their modern-day archetypal equivalents:

> Russia annexes the Crimea. **Confucius** suits up and heads to the White House to request action.
>
> **Obama** @44thPresident
> Go ask Congress for authorization.

In the same vein, we transform the oftentimes alienating cultural setting of each conversation to situations more familiar, making the dialog more relevant and more engaging. This we do in *Analects* 3.17, which features a "Declaration of the New Moon" ceremony as backdrop:

> Zigong wanted to dispense with the sacrifice of a live sheep at the Declaration of the New Moon ceremony. The Master said: "Zigong, you grudge the sheep—I, ritual propriety."[3]

To prevent what is in the mind of the English language reader an outlandish ceremony from hijacking the exchange, we graft these very ideas onto a traditional American holiday, thereby redirecting the reader back to the message's humanist core:

> **Sly** @Woodstock
> What do you say we put an end to the slaughter of turkeys on Thanksgiving Day?
>
> **Confucius** @the_master
> You're sad to see the birds die — I get that, but the alternative is to kill off a venerated American tradition. Now that, I cannot live with.

---

[2] See Reiss, Katharina, and Hans J. Vermeer. 1984. *Grundlegung einer allgemeinen Translationastheorie*, p.19. Tübingen: Max Niemeyer Verlag.

[3] From Ames, Roger T., and Henry Rosemont Jr. 1998. *The Analects of Confucius: A Philosophical Translation*, p.86. New York: Ballantine.

The reader will notice also that the discourses of Confucius in this book are presented in a unique format — that of the instant messaging feed — and for good reason. For one, the language of the *Analects* is conversational in nature — the short remarks and casual comments that form the bulk of the work lend themselves well to the conventions of texts and tweets. But more importantly, the use of text messages allows us to identify each participant using a meaningful user handle: we assign to every participant a name is that is image-rich and semantically-transparent, just as they appear to readers of Chinese.

Here we must point out that the experience of the casual reader perusing Confucius in English is markedly different from that of the East Asian reader skimming through the text in Chinese *hanzi*, Japanese *kanji*, or Korean *hanja* in a number of ways, the most significant being that names composed of block characters pregnant with meaning are inevitably reduced to semantically opaque random syllables in the English romanization process. The *Analects* documents exchanges between Confucius and dozens of disciples and contemporaries, the names of whom often provide clues to the quirks and idiosyncrasies of the individual. Any educated Asian reader would be able to see that the character *lù* (路) in the name of the disciple Zǐlù (子路) means "walkway", and that the character *xià* (夏) in the name of the disciple Zǐxià (子夏) means "summer" — a disciple who, at times in the *Analects*, is referred to by his birth name Shāng (商), which means "merchant". As illustrated above, a mental image is created for each personality in the mind of the reader accessing the text through block characters, which aids in memory retention and reading comprehension. To the English language reader however, the list of random syllables is long: Zǐlù, Zǐxià, Zǐyóu, Zǐzhāng, Zǐgòng, Zǐyóu, Zǐhuá, Zǐwǒ…all similar sounding due to the lack of imagery associated with each sound, turning the Chinese classic into a work populated by characters barely distinguishable from each other.

Which is why we use handles instead of transliterations.

So instead of Zǐlù we have **Louie** @Walker; instead of Zǐxià we have **Auguste** @LeMerchant, allowing the imagery of "walkway", "summer", and "merchant" to shine through, creating an effect that better approximates the reading experience of the source language reader.

At some point the reader may wonder whether a translation of the *Analects* which removes all vestiges of Chineseness is sufficiently authentic. On this issue, we take a page from the writings of Bulgarian linguist Sider Florin:

> If we strip a cowboy of his traditional garb and attire him in the burnous of a Sahara shepherd he will lose all his natural semblance and turn into an Arab. If we make a geisha change her loose and airy kimono for a Tyrolean dirndl with a close fitting bodice there will be nothing Japanese left in her.[4]

But such cultural transformations are necessary in order to create an authentic experience. The cultural peculiarities that appear on the pages of the *Analects* do not at first appear to pose a problem and may even strike some as pleasantly exotic. But as the foreignness piles on, the cumulative effect of multiple layers of unfamiliarity eventually reaches a point where it impedes reading and hinders comprehension. In the *Analects*, Confucius talks about elaborate temple rites replete with ornate ritual and animal sacrifice, which must strike the modern reader as excessive, but in Confucius's day was as proper and necessary as showing up for work in a suit and tie. Many of Confucius's metaphors are built around the objects and activities of his time: the wheels and axles of horse carriages, the hardiness of pines and firs, the practice of archery and the consumption of rice wine — objects and activities which, while recognizable to the modern reader, may not have the same significance — hence the

---

[4] Florin, Sider. 1993. "Realia in Translation". In Palma Zlateva and Andre Lefevere, eds., *Translation as Social Action: Russian and Bulgarian Perspectives*, p.123. London: Routledge.

comprehension gap.

French translation theorist André Lefevere explains that:

> Translation, though based in language, is by no means limited to language. Translators have to transfer things and concepts from one universe of reference to another, not just words from one language to another.[5]

This "transfer of things and concepts" is what we have done in our translation. Thus in *Analects* 14.06, when Yì (羿) and Ào (奡) are given as examples of generals who strike fear into the hearts of their enemies, we replace the characters with Napoleon and Hitler. In *Analects* 3.07, the consumption of rice wine after an archery match is replaced with the drinking of beer after a ball game. Throughout the dialogs, service to the emperor is recast as the more relatable experience of working in government or reporting to one's superior in the workplace.

Two key notions lie at the heart of Confucius's world view, namely, that of *rén* (仁) and that of the *jūnzǐ* (君子). The challenge for the translator lies in the absence of words in English matching the broad semantic scope covered by each of these terms — any word chosen to translate these concepts is going to be an imprecise one, the choice being between the lesser of many possible evils. In academic translations which seek to impose a one-to-one lexical mapping between Chinese and English, *rén* is regularly rendered as "altruism", "compassion", or "humanity". The problem however is that while in one context "compassion" might work better, in another "humanity" may actually produce the more natural reading, and there are yet other contexts where only a linguistic or cultural paraphrase will do. In this book we abandon the notion of one-to-one isomorphism and choose to translate key concepts differently each time according to context — not the preferred method of scholars who may wish to

---

[5] Ibid, p.122.

understand how many times and in what contexts a particular turn of phrase is used, but immensely liberating for the casual reader who simply wishes to get to the crux of Confucius's message. Similarly, we do not adopt the traditional translation of "gentleman" for *jūnzǐ* for the reason that the term smacks of dated etiquette and creates a distance between text and reader which is absent in Confucius's use of the word. We choose instead to adopt variable, context-appropriate renderings of *jūnzǐ*, which appears in different passages as "guys", "good guys", "good people", "capable people", "good men", "worthy men", "men of class", "accomplished individuals", "well-rounded individuals", "persons of integrity", and other contextual variants.

By making a conscious decision to privilege naturalness over literalness, we also allow ourselves the means to preserve the meter and music of the original, which, more often than not, is lost in English. While the language of the Chinese classics is typically concise and rhythmic, rich with symbolism and parallelisms, often having the ring of poetry, it is rarely so in translation. With a few notable exceptions in Ezra Pound and Arthur Waley, these metrical properties of the source language rarely carry over into English; rather, the majority of translations resort to accurate but odd turns of phrase that make the text read more like a philosophical treatise than a conversational exchange.

In choosing to focus on readability and produce a reader-oriented translation of the *Analects*, we have been careful not to neglect the sizeable body of scholarship that has been amassed on the subject and present an interpretation that is both current and theoretically-informed. We take into account interpretations advanced by both classical and modern scholars as well as textual variants found in manuscripts uncovered from the grottoes of Dūnhuáng, and, more recently, newly discovered archeological fragments from pre-Christian era tombs in Dìngzhōu, Guōdiàn, and various other excavation sites unearthed in the past half century. The result is an understanding of this Confucian classic that may, in some instances, differ from those found in received readings in Asia.

A case in point is the opening passage of the *Analects*, which, in most translations takes the form of three disjointed exclamations:

> Studying, and from time to time going over what you've learned — that's enjoyable, isn't it? To have friends come from a long way off — that's a pleasure, isn't it? Others don't understand him, but he doesn't resent it — that's the true gentleman, isn't it?[6]

A closer look into historical usage however will reveal that the three statements are in fact related and logically sequential. The key lies in the interpretation of the character *péng* 朋, which in modern Chinese cannot stand alone but must occur in the expression *péngyou* 朋友 "friend". In writings from the Eastern Zhou (771-221 B.C.) however, *péng* 朋 is an independent morpheme and means something very different from "friend", as is also evident from the construction of the character itself, with two human forms placed side by side — the meaning of *péng* 朋 is "peer", or, to be more precise, a peer in the pursuit of knowledge — i.e., a classmate or fellow academic.

Along the same lines, in the first statement *xué* 學 "to learn" is not the same as *xí* 習 "to practice", the distinction between which has become muddled in modern usage. And the adverbial element *shí* 時 "time", which has been interpreted variously as "constantly" (i.e., "time after time"), "seasonally" (i.e., "with the passing of time"), or "opportunity" (e.g., "at the right time"), makes sense only when taken in the sense of finding the right occasion to apply what one has learned — the only one of the three options that is remotely enjoyable in any way. It is hard to imagine how, as traditional interpretations would have it,

---

[6] Watson, Burton. 2007. *The Analects of Confucius*, p.16. New York: Columbia University Press.

"studying and from time to time going over what you've learned" can be, for the average student, a pleasurable experience.

With these pieces in place, the entire passage can then be interpreted as three sequential stages in the acquisition of knowledge: the first stage involves the pleasure of learning something new and finding ways to apply the newly acquired knowledge; the second stage involves the sharing of experiences with an inner circle of those in the know, i.e., specialists and fellow enthusiasts who share a love for the discipline; the final stage is a state in which the level of knowledge is so specialized that few laymen can appreciate its worth, yet therein lies its exclusive appeal.

Another example is *Analects* 15.39 "have education, no categorization" (有教無類), believed by many to exemplify Confucius's non-discriminatory stance on education. Most Asian textbooks today insert a first person "I" into the sentence, producing a descriptive reading of the passage:

> My teaching is addressed to all indifferently.[7]

This traditional reading however does not square with current scholarship on the syntax of the Eastern Zhōu, which favors a conditional reading, namely, "with access to education, differences in background fade away", removing the speaker from the picture and turning the quote into a phenomenological statement[8]. A number of other readings have sprung up over the ages, including that of exhortation — "when you evaluate people, look only at their educational achievement and not at their social or racial background"[9], that of innate nature —

---

[7] Simon Leys. 1997. *The Analects of Confucius*, p.79. New York: W.W. Norton.

[8] See Liú, Guó Píng. 2002. "'Yǒujiào Wúlèi' as a Phenomenological Statement Rather Than as a Statement of Confucius's Educational Ideal". *Yánjiù yǔ Dòngtài* (Da Yeh University Center for Liberal Arts) 7: 11-19.

[9] Ibid.

"when you educate someone, they become good regardless of how they were before"[10], and that of educational method — "when you educate people, don't box them into rigid categories, but let their minds wander freely"[11]. The terseness of the classical Chinese language makes these different interpretations possible, and the paths that these Confucian adages have traveled through ancient, medieval, and pre-modern history have only enriched their content and added to the contexts through which we can appreciate their application.

The early twenty-first century has yielded important new finds in the archaeology of the Confucian *Analects*. While textual variants of the *Analects*, each of differing lengths, flourished in the Han dynasty, today we are left with all but one, based on the twenty-chapter synthesis of Marquis Zhāng Yǔ 張禹 (d. 5 B.C.). Thanks to the popularity of the Marquis's compilation during the reign of his protégé Emperor Chéng (51-7 B.C.), the all-important Lǔ and Qí recensions, from which the synthesis was originally constructed, each with additional chapters, have been lost to the pages of history. That is, until 2016, when fragments believed to form the twenty-second chapter of the Qí *Analects* were unearthed from the Han dynasty tomb of Marquis Liú Hè 劉賀 (92-69 B.C.) in present-day Jiāngxī province. Subsequently, similar texts were identified in the excavation site of the Hàn dynasty fortification at Jiānshuǐ Jīnguān 肩水金關 (121-102 B.C.) in the Gobi Desert, which in turn led academics to fragments from the twenty-first chapter of the Qí *Analects*, giving us, for the first time, a glimpse into the two remaining chapters of the *Analects*. These chapter fragments are translated for the first time into English in this book.

As we have shown, despite having formed the backbone

---

[10] Zhāng, Sōnghuī. 1989. "An Alternative Reading of 'Yǒujiào Wúlèi'". *Qilu Journal* 1989 (6): 93-94.

[11] Zhāng, Chōng 2013. "An Alternative Reading of 'Yǒujiào Wúlèi'". *Journal of Dezhou University* 29 (3): 62-64.

of East Asian moral thinking for close to two millennia, the language and the interpretation of the Confucian canon is by no means static, as the words of the Master are constantly being infused with new life to suit the needs of different times. Here we present yet another incarnation of these beloved discourses, and in a thoroughly revamped medium and format at that — one with which the contemporary reader would hopefully be more at ease, so that the words of Confucius the Master survive not as historical ephemera, but as timeless wisdom that can be applied comfortably to the here and now.

— CHRIS WEN-CHAO LI, D.PHIL.
Professor of Linguistics, San Francisco State University

Preface by Frederik H. Green

What *did* Confucius really say? Confucius is one of the few universal philosophical and cultural figures whose name, along with the names of Socrates and Jesus, Muhammad and Shakespeare, Buddha and Kant, no longer seems to require an explanation, regardless of where or in which context it is uttered. Not only is this the case in China, Japan and Korea, where Confucius has had a profound impact on the development of those countries' respective societies, but it is also the case in the West, where Confucius has fascinated philosophers and general readers ever since he was first introduced by Jesuit translators in the seventeenth century. Recognizing the cultural centrality of Master Kong (孔子, 551-479 B.C.), as Confucius is known in Chinese, the Jesuits honored Confucius by bestowing him a Latinized version of his name (instead of simply transcribing it phonetically) and translated many of the texts that form the Confucian canon, namely works that were allegedly either anthologized by Confucius himself, such as the *Book of Odes* (《詩經》 , 1100-700 B.C.), works that represent the thought of Confucius' later disciples, such as *Mencius* (《孟子》 , 372-289 B.C.), and works that are directly based on the teachings of Confucius, such as *The Analects*. Known as the "Lunyü" (《論語》) in Chinese, which literally means "Discussions," *The Analects* have also come to be known as *The Sayings of Confucius* or *The Wisdom of Confucius* in the English-speaking world, depending on which of the dozens of existing translations is consulted. *The Analects* consist of a collection of a few hundred statements attributed to Confucius as well as dialogues between Confucius and his disciples, who are also credited with posthumously anthologizing them. They range from topics such as the value and function of education and the importance of tradition and ritual to friendship, warfare, proper conduct and statecraft. *The Analects* are believed to date to the Warring States period (475–221 B.C.), but it was only during the Han dynasty (206 B.C.–220 A.D.) that they were elevated to the status of canonical texts. In later centuries, knowledge of Confucian texts, including *The Analects*, became essential for success in the Civil Service exams (科舉), and Confucian ideas on statehood, ritual, ancestor worship, education, and societal hierarchies have exerted lasting influences on East Asian societies.

So what did Confucius really say in those lines that are allegedly his own words? In China, this question has led to an immense corpus of commentaries, in addition to original works by scholars and philosophers who wished to shed light on or reinterpret the words of Confucius. Interpretations of *The Analects* in China and other parts of East Asia have never been static, but have greatly changed and evolved over time according to political or societal circumstances, and interestingly, continue to do so today. The same can be said of the reception of *The Analects* in the West. If Jesuit translations and commentaries led to an idealization of the Confucian bureaucracy among Enlightenment thinkers such as Gottfried Wilhelm Leibniz (1646-1716) and Jean-Jacques Rousseau (1712-1778), Confucian values and thought were frequently cited by Western "China-hands" in the 19th century as the primary reasons for China's decline after the country's often painful encounters with Western modernity, especially in the wake of China's defeat in the Opium Wars (1839-42 & 1856-60). But it wasn't only self-proclaimed China experts in the West who blamed Confucius for China's mounting problems. Chinese intellectuals of the early 20th century, such as the famous writer Lu Xun (魯迅, 1881-1936), came to be believe that Chinese superstition, bigotry, and an aversion to progress were all caused by the teaching of Confucian values. In Lu Xun's famous novella "Diary of a Madman" (《狂人日記》, 1918), these values were even equated with a form of cannibalism: when reading the classics, the protagonist suddenly sees the words "eat people" (吃人) appear between the lines. The belief that classical Chinese social and ethical philosophy was no longer compatible with the demands of the present was shared by the Chinese Communist Party, which declared Confucius an enemy of the people in the wake of the founding of the People's Republic in 1949, and in subsequent years, the legacy of Confucius was systematically deemphasized. In contrast, Chiang Kai-shek's Nationalist government, after retreating to Taiwan in 1949, re-emphasized adherence to Confucian principles to give weight to the claim that it was the only legitimate government to rule over China. Consequently, the study of Confucian texts continued to be part of the school curriculum. However, as Taiwanese society modernized and became increasingly drawn to Western values, Confucius' pre-eminence likewise began to fade.

So, who still cares about what Confucius really said? Interest in Confucius (and in traditional culture in general) has seen a striking revival, both in mainland China and in Taiwan. Fashioning itself as the heir to China's glorious dynastic past, the Chinese Communist Party has in recent years resurrected Confucius as a Chinese "saint". Not only did the opening ceremony of the Beijing Olympics in 2008 feature a Zhou-dynasty inspired drum-dance and a recital of selected quotes from *The Analects*, but since 2004, hundreds of government-funded Confucius Institutes have sprung up on university campuses all over the world to offer instruction in Chinese language and classical culture. At the same time, the general Chinese public has developed an intense curiosity for what Confucius really said, resulting in hundreds of new editions of *The Analects*, ranging from meticulously annotated scholarly editions to lavishly decorated volumes printed on silk and sold in cloth-bound cases. Meanwhile, Yu Dan (于丹,

1965), professor of media studies at China's Beijing Normal University, gained fame in 2006 with a lecture series entitled "Yu Dan's Insights into the Analects" (于丹《論語》心得) that sold at least 4 million copies (and possibly twice as many in pirated versions). In Taiwan, the well-known writer and art-critic Jiang Xun (蔣勳, 1947) has generated tremendous interest in traditional culture via his publicly broadcasted lectures and numerous essays and books, some of which likewise attempt to make Confucius more relevant and accessible to contemporary readers. In the West, scholars and journalists frequently draw on Confucius and the Confucian legacy to explain practically any social phenomenon that can be observed in China today, from its meteoritic rise since the 1990s to its embrace of authoritarianism and resistance to democratization. Even the alleged superiority of Chinese-American students in mathematics has been linked to Confucius's emphasis of the value of education.

What did Confucius really say, hence, clearly is a question in urgent need of an answer. Sadly, most existing English translations of *The Analects* provide only little assistance in the quest to understand the true meaning of Confucius's utterances. While scholarly translations often attempt to recreate the archaic ring of the original and are frequently littered with pages of footnotes and complex explanations, popular translations tend to gloss over the historical significance of the many allusions and references in *The Analects* or trivialize the text's core meaning. The present translation by Professor Chris Wen-chao Li is unique in its approach. Highly readable and often outrightly funny, it is nevertheless based on meticulous linguistic research and distinguishes itself through its depth of historical coverage. Li achieves this fusion of readability and profundity by adopting a goal-oriented functional approach to translation in which core concepts and historical figures are not transcribed and explained in lengthy footnotes or commentaries, but replaced with time- or place-specific equivalents. A reference to a statesman from the age of Confucius becomes a reference to Al Gore or Bill Clinton in Li's translation, while references to ancient kings are replaced by names of rulers of European antiquity or the Middle Ages. The same is done to proper names of important individuals. Lin Fang (林放), a contemporary of Confucius with expert knowledge on official protocol, becomes **Pierre Larousse** @Encyclopedie in Li's translation. The China of Confucius's age is typically replaced with present-day America, and the challenges society faced during the Waring States period are replaced with global warming and immigration.

Few scholars are more qualified to offer a convincing answer to the question of what Confucius really did say than Chris Wen-chao Li. A professor of Chinese at San Francisco State University, Li received his early schooling in the United States and completed college in Taiwan before going to the United Kingdom, where he was awarded a doctorate in linguistics from Oxford University. Not only is Li fully bi-lingual and bi-cultural, he also possesses expert knowledge of Chinese historical syntax and phonology and is familiar with the textual history of the Confucian and Western classics. In addition, Li is blessed with a wonderful sense of humor, which not only adds to the pleasure of reading his version of *The Analects*, but also turns Confucius into an infinitely more approachable character. Confucius in Li's translation at times curses his critics and extols the beauty of Beethoven's and Madonna's music. He also urges his disciples to remember his maxims "as if they're written on your forehead or printed on your bumper sticker" — upon which one disciple ends up tattooing them on his arm.

So what did Confucius really say? Li ultimately provides the curious reader with an answer that will satisfy the scholar and general reader alike. It will delight students of Western philosophy (Confucius pays a visit to Diogenes of Sinope) as much as US history buffs (Confucius speaks to White House Chief-of-Staff Henry Halleck and asks after Abraham Lincoln) and basketball fans (Why was dunk legend Julius Erving of the Philadelphia 76ers called "Doctor J"?). With its short but highly insightful footnotes,

the book will also satisfy those who seek to understand
The Analects in their socio-historical context and those
who want to learn more about Chinese culture and
civilization. Throughout the work, Li skillfully demystifies
Confucius. It becomes clear in the end that to make sense
of Confucius' words, one requires neither a PhD in Asian
civilization nor has to spend years living in China. This
translation of *The Analects* is a game changer. It provides
all of us who teach Confucianism with an invaluable tool
that will help us disseminate the moral message of Master
Kong. It will also allow readers to weigh in when the media
cites Confucius in their China reporting and to see through
Chinese politicians when they refer to *The Analects* to
justify dubious policy choices. Finally, Li's translation
makes it clear that the wisdom of Confucius is just as
relevant now as it is was in Confucius' own time, for who
would disagree with his utterance that "you'd be surprised
how far an education and some coaching in etiquette
would get you in life."

— FREDERIK H. GREEN, PH.D.
Associate Professor of Chinese, San Francisco State University

Technical Notes

The source text used for this translation is based in large part on the third century compilation *Lúnyǔ Jíjiě* 《論語集解》 of Wèi dynasty scholar Hé Yàn (何晏, 195-249 A.D.). In addition, textual variants found in manuscripts uncovered from the grottoes of Dūnhuáng, and, more recently, newly discovered archeological fragments from pre-Christian era tombs in Dìngzhōu, Guōdiàn, and other excavation sites unearthed in the past half century are compared to arrive at plausible and coherent readings.

In addition, where the received text appears to be scrambled or inconsistent, such as in Sections 12.10 and 16.12, we adopt extrapolations and rearrangements proposed by Chén (1986)[1], and in Sections 6.1 and 6.2 we introduce content from texts traditionally categorized as "Analects At Large" 《逸論語》 believed by many to be quoted from long-lost earlier recensions of the *Analects*, fragments of which are recorded in historical and philological writings passed down through other lineages.

In Chapters 21 and 22, we reconstruct the lost chapters of the Qí *Analects* based on bamboo slips recovered from the Hàn dynasty tomb of the Marquis of Hǎihūn (92-69 B.C.) and additional fragments unearthed at the Hàn dynasty fortification of Jiānshuǐ Jīnguān 肩水金關 (121-102 B.C.) in the Gobi Desert, which were made public for the first time in early 2016.

---

[1] Chen, Shih-chuan. 1986. *The Confucian Analects: A New Translation of the Corrected Text of Lun Yü*. Taipei: Li Ming Cultural Enterprise.

The earliest received texts of the *Analects* were not numbered, although they appear to be grouped into sections that correspond closely to the numbered arrangements of contemporary editions. Fragments of the *Analects* unearthed from Hàn dynasty tombs also appear to support section divisions, with each section beginning at the top of a new slip of bamboo.

Since the nineteenth century, a number of different numbering systems have been proposed to label the passages of the *Analects*, the earliest being that of British sinologist James Legge (1815-1897), whose system appears in his masterwork *The Chinese Classics: With a Translation, Critical and Exegetical Notes, Prolegomena, and Copious Indexes* (London: Trubner, 1861). Other notable arrangements include the Harvard-Yenching Institute's *Concordance to the Analects of Confucius* 《論語引得》 (Beijing, 1940) and that of Chinese linguist Yáng Bójùn (楊伯峻), used in his book *Lúnyǔ Yìzhù* 《論語譯注》 [Annotated and Translated Analects] (Beijing: Zhonghua Book Co.,1958).

The numbering system adopted in the present work is for the most part based on that of Yáng (1958) with the exception of Chapters 8, 14, and 20. In Chapter 8, we follow Chén (1986) in dividing what is traditionally *Analects* 8.02 into two thematically-distinct sections. For Chapter 14, we adopt the 47-part chapter division of Legge (1861). In Chapter 20, we replicate Chén's (1986) division of the three traditional sections into seven groupings based on topical affinity.

ROMANIZATION

In the footnotes and introductory sections of this book, the transliteration of personal and place names from the Chinese follows the Hanyu Pinyin system of romanization, with tone marks represented as diacritics above the nuclear vowel of each full-toned syllable.

Where, for purposes of comparison, passages of the *Analects* are quoted from the translations of other authors, the romanization scheme used by the quoted author is preserved in its entirety— no attempt is made to convert the transliterations of quoted texts into the Hanyu Pinyin system adopted in this book.

ALTERNATIVE TRANSLATIONS

Throughout this book, where cultural elements have been altered, transformed, abridged, or deleted, an alternative translation that follows the source text more closely is provided in the form of a commentary. Unless otherwise indicated, all translations that appear in the commentary sections (including preface and footnotes) are my own.

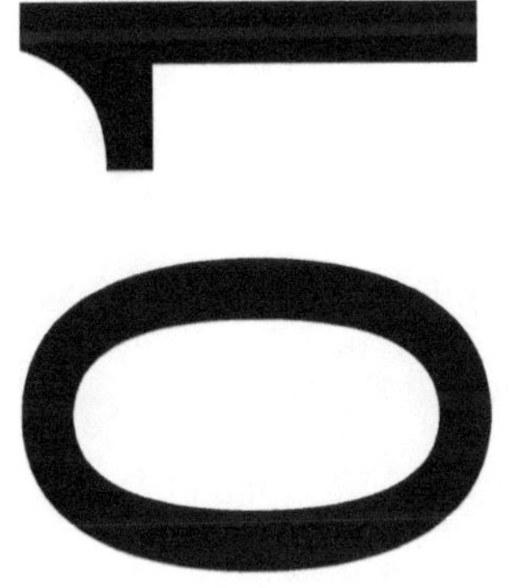

LEARNING

學而

Confucius @MasterSays
Learning and having occasion to apply your knowledge — how cool is that? Keeping company with visitors who share your passion — how sweet is that? Not caring when the world thinks nothing of your talent — how classy is that?

§ Session 01.01

Hubert @EubieSays
A guy who treats his family right is not going to screw things up at work; a guy who doesn't screw things up at work is not going to go rob a bank. You see, you've got to start from the basics. Once the basics are taken care of, things will fall into place. And I say, there's nothing more basic than taking care of family.

§ Session 01.02

Confucius @MasterSays
Guys who talk sweet and smile all the time are scum.

§ Session 01.03

Jonathan @JonoSays
Not a day goes by that I don't ask myself: Am I a letdown to my boss? Am I drifting apart from my friends? Am I falling behind in my studies?

§ Session 01.04

Confucius @MasterSays
To be a small-time politician you need to look the part: show dedication and be a man of your word; keep costs down and look after your constituents; introduce unpopular measures only as a last resort.

§ Session 01.05

Confucius @MasterSays
Kids these days need to learn to behave at home and be polite in the company of strangers. A bit of modesty would help, as would a lesson in honesty and the need to respect the rights of others. And when they have time on their hands, read, read, read!

§ Session 01.06

Auguste @LeMerchant
When you get the type of guy who's like taking care of his elderly parents and working his pants off for his boss, and all his friends take him seriously — guys like that, I'd say they've made it in life, even if they don't have a piece of paper to prove it.

§ Session 01.07

Confucius @MasterSays
If you don't look the part, you won't be taken seriously — so get an education to polish off those rough edges. Be a man of your word. Make friends in higher circles, and be willing to learn from your mistakes.

§ Session 01.08

Jonathan @JonoSays
Show respect for the dead, and you'll be worth more in people's eyes.

§ Session 01.09

Efron @Ziskind
When the master arrives in a new place, he always has the lowdown on the local movers and shakers. How does he do it? I mean, does he go around prying, or do people freely offer up the juicy tidbits?

Sly @Woodstock
When you see in your midst a celebrity of such great stature, appearing so personable and so willing to lend a sympathetic ear, how could you not but want to spill your guts out to him? He has no need to pry. It is his affable persona that invites strangers to share their most intimate secrets. This is what distinguishes him from your garden-variety paparazzi.

§ Session 01.10

Confucius @MasterSays
Watch what a guy says when his old man's around, and then see what he's up to when the father's no longer on top of things. Cuz you see, my idea of a good son is one who takes over the family business, and, three years on, out of respect for the father, has no intention whatsoever of changing the way things are run.

§ Session 01.11

Hubert @EubieSays
Laws are there to keep the peace. That is the wisdom of our founding fathers. Nothing escapes the reach of the law. While it is tempting to strike deals outside the letter of the law, such shady dealings rarely ever see happy endings.

§ Session 01.12

Hubert @EubieSays
Only promise what is within reason — that way you're more likely to make good on your word. Show courtesy but don't go over the top — that way you're less likely to be taken for a joke. When you're down-to-earth and unassuming, people are better able to relate to you.

§ Session 01.13

Confucius @MasterSays
It's not about what you eat or where you live, it's about doing the right thing, using the right word, and hanging out with the right people. That's what progress is all about.

§ Session 01.14

Sly @Woodstock
What do you think of those who are poor but not resentful, or rich but not snooty?

Confucius @MasterSays
They're admirable, but wouldn't you rather be poor but proud, or rich but using wealth towards a good end?

Sly @Woodstock
You're right. When luck smiles on you, pay it forward; when life gives you lemons, make lemonade[1], isn't that so?

Confucius @MasterSays
You've read my mind. I couldn't have put it better myself.

§ Session 01.15

Confucius @MasterSays
So no one has the faintest idea what you're going through. Big deal. Like, do you have any idea what other people are going through?

§ Session 01.16

---

[1] Source text quotes a line from the lyric "Qí River Bend", collected in the *Book of Songs*, Airs of Wèi, No. 1: "Like chipping and chiseling / Like sanding and smoothing", describing the work of a jade artisan, meant as a metaphor for a literary scholar striving for perfection.

2

SERVICE

為政

Confucius @MasterSays
When, in politics, you follow your conscience, you'll shine like the brightest star in the sky while heavenly bodies rally around you.

§ Session 02.01

Confucius @MasterSays
When it comes to the verses of the Old Testament[1], you can count on one thing: they'll blow your mind.

§ Session 02.02

Confucius @MasterSays
Where order depends on law and the fear of punishment, people are opportunistic and unscrupulous; where peace is rooted in civility and the exchange of good will, citizens are forthright and conscientious.

§ Session 02.03

---

[1] Source text addresses not the Old Testament but the ancient Chinese *Book of Songs* — a classic in its own day.

Confucius @MasterSays
I devoured the classics at age fifteen and by thirty was at the top of my game; not until forty though was I completely rid of self-doubt, and come fifty, I could sense my purpose in life. In my sixties I grew more tolerant of different views, and now at seventy I am finally able to speak my mind, this time without fear of offending any sensibilities.

§ Session 02.04

Cesare de Borgia seeks advice on being a good son.

Confucius @MasterSays
Don't go against your parents' wishes.

 Later that day, with **Francis** at the wheel, **Confucius** recounts the earlier conversation.

Confucius @MasterSays
So Cesare de Borgia came by today and asked how to be a good son. I said don't go against your parents' wishes.

Francis @Waite
Meaning what?

Confucius @MasterSays
Meaning treat them with dignity when they're alive, and when they're no longer of this world, show them a proper burial and say prayers in their name.

§ Session 02.05

Rodrigo de Borgia asks how to be a good son.

Confucius @MasterSays
Give your parents little cause for worry save for their deteriorating health.

§ Session 02.06

Yanni asks how to be a good son.

Confucius @MasterSays
Nowadays, it's like if you give your parents food and shelter, you're doing them a big favor. I mean, you'd do the same for your dog, wouldn't you? Unless you show them some respect, what difference is there, really?

§ Session 02.07

Auguste asks how to be a good son.

Confucius @MasterSays
It's all in the look, in the expression of intimacy. Don't for a minute think that if you wine and dine them and tend to their every need that you've fulfilled your familial duties.

§ Session 02.08

Confucius @MasterSays
I've been talking to Owen all day and he doesn't say a thing, like he's stupid or something. But I go away and, boom, he does everything just the way I told him to. The guy's not stupid.

§ Session 02.09

Confucius @MasterSays
Watch a man's every move, ask why he's behaving that way, and look for signs of unease. That way no one can ever hide anything from you.

§ Session 02.10

Confucius @MasterSays
If, when you go over old material, you find yourself exploring the issue from new angles, you know you've mastered the subject matter.

§ Session 02.11

Confucius @MasterSays
Don't be a tool.

§ Session 02.12

Sly asks how to be worth more in the eyes of other people.

Confucius @MasterSays
Do it first and *then* go tell people about it.

§ Session 02.13

Confucius @MasterSays
Guys get along without exchanging favors; wimps exchange favors but don't get along.

§ Session 02.14

Confucius @MasterSays
Learning that leaves no room for speculation is suspect; speculation that is not informed by learning is wacko.

§ Session 02.15

Confucius @MasterSays
When you discriminate against people who are different from you, you're the one who is losing out.

§ Session 02.16

Confucius @MasterSays
I'll tell you what it means to know something. If you know it you know it; if you don't you don't. That's what I call really knowing.

§ Session 02.17

Ezra asks how to move up the corporate ladder.

Confucius @MasterSays
Listen to what is said, leave out what doesn't make sense, then comment on the rest — that way you're less likely to offend other people. Watch how things are done, leave out what goes against your beliefs, then do what you can — that way you have fewer misgivings. If you have few misgivings and don't offend other people, chances are you'll be appreciated for your work.

§ Session 02.18

 **King Maximilian** seeks better approval ratings.

Confucius @MasterSays
Deliver crooks into the hands of honest citizens and people are happy; deliver upright citizens into the hands of criminals and all hell breaks loose.

§ Session 02.19

Cosimo de Medici @ilGrande
How do you get people to respect you, to be loyal to you, and to be motivated to work for you?

Confucius @MasterSays
Carry yourself with dignity and they'll respect you; treat them well and they'll be loyal to you; promote the capable and teach the unskilled, and they'll be motivated to work for you.

§ Session 02.20

 **Confucius** is asked if it has ever occurred to him to take up political causes.

Confucius @MasterSays
"Liberté, égalité, fraternité" was the battle cry of the French Revolution. As president of my fraternity, I granted equality to all pledges and safeguarded their liberty in the pursuit of happiness[2]. If that isn't standing up for a worthy cause, I'm not sure what is.

§ Session 02.21

---

[2] Confucius often deliberately misquotes from classic sources to give what can only be described as a glib reply to questions that appear to cast him in a negative light. In this exchange, he is asked why he chooses not to enter into politics, the answer to which should have been that his obsession with the moral high ground put him at odds with the political masters of the day. But Confucius deftly avoids embarrassment by quoting from the *Book of Documents*, "Performing familial duties and practicing brotherly love, in effect, contributes to the body politic," to deflect accusations that he is apolitical.

Confucius @MasterSays
When a man has no credibility, anything goes. It's like a wagon that's lost a wheel or a car that's blown a tire — you have no idea which way it's going to swerve.

§ Session 02.22

Ezra @Johnson
What would the world look like generations from now?

Confucius @MasterSays
Greece paved the way for Rome, and Rome shaped the civilizations in our midst[3]. If anything was to succeed our modern civilization, would it be hard to guess where it would get its inspiration?

§ Session 02.23

Confucius @MasterSays
When you go out of your way to please[4], you're a spineless invertebrate; when you can lend a hand but don't, you're a gutless wimp.

§ Session 02.24

---

[3] Source text makes reference to the pre-imperial Three Dynasties of Xià (2207-1766 B.C.), Shāng (1765-1122 B.C.), and Zhōu (1121-249 B.C.), describing how the traditions of the Xià shaped those of the Shāng, and how Shāng traditions were subsequently adopted by the Zhōu.

[4] Source text: "When you worship ancestral spirits that are not your own…"

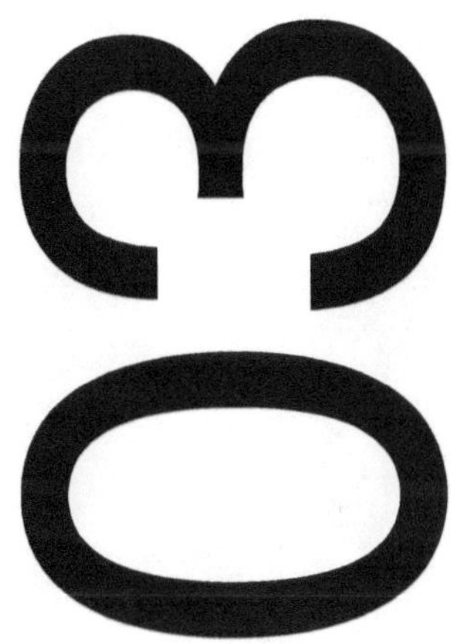

DANCE

八佾

President **Bill Clinton** enjoys a striptease in the Oval Office[1].

Confucius @MasterSays
If that isn't inappropriate, I don't know what is.

§ Session 03.01

Pentagon employees use government-issue charge cards to pay for adult entertainment[2].

Confucius @MasterSays
What part of "For Government Use Only" do they not understand?

§ Session 03.02

---

[1] Source text: "The head of the Jì clan had eight rows of eight dancers (a format reserved for the emperor alone) perform in his own courtyard."

[2] Source text describes how, at the conclusion of a sacrificial rite, feudal clans brazenly perform the imperial Yōng hymn from the *Book of Songs*, reserved exclusively for the emperor. Here, Confucius quotes from the hymn the line "The princes stand in wait as the emperor looks on" to show that only the emperor is entitled to the use of the hymn.

Confucius @MasterSays
What use is good dress sense when you're a wolf in sheep's clothing? What good are angelic graces when they're a front for demonic perversions?[3]

§ Session 03.03

 **Pierre Larousse** asks what basic human instincts lie at the root of civilized behavior.

Confucius @MasterSays
Great question. The idea is to curb your excesses in day-to-day living, but to let it all out when mourning the dead.

§ Session 03.04

Confucius @MasterSays
Leaders in Asia and Africa still command an aura of respect, whereas American presidents[4] of late have become the laughing stock of the world.

§ Session 03.05

---

[3] Source text comments that music and ritual propriety are a mere façade when he who practices them does not have it in him to do good.

[4] Source text: "The barbarians of the East (Yí) and the North (Dí) still hold their rulers in awe, unlike the people of the Chinese states."

 Permission is granted to big oil companies to drill near Glacier National Park. **Confucius** grills **Randall** of the Environmental Protection Agency[5].

Confucius @MasterSays
Is there nothing you can do?

Randall @RandSays
I'm afraid not.

Confucius @MasterSays
The U.S. Forest Service might turn a blind eye, but do you think Mother Nature[6] would really stand for this kind of transgression?

§ Session 03.06

Confucius @MasterSays
Guys don't get physical except in sports. Even then, they'd slap each other on the back before the game, and all go out for a beer when it's over[7]. There's sportsmanship for you.

§ Session 03.07

---

[5] Source text describes the head of the Jì clan performing ritual sacrifice on Mount Tai — a holy site to which access is reserved for the emperor.

[6] Source text: "Do you really believe the Gods of Mount Tai would be less knowledgeable in these matters than Lín Fàng?" (NOTE: Lín Fàng, a.k.a. **Pierre Larousse** @Encyclopedie (see Session 03.04), is a contemporary of Confucius with expert knowledge on official protocol).

[7] Source text uses the example of archery for sport and has the contenders "bow and defer to one another" before each game.

Auguste @LeMerchant
What is the meaning behind "Starry, starry night, paint your palette blue and gray, look out on a summer's day with eyes that know the darkness in my soul"?[8]

Confucius @MasterSays
It is about an artist who tries to "sketch the trees and the daffodils"[9], and "catch the breeze and the winter chills in colors on the snowy linen land".

Auguste @LeMerchant
And how "weathered faces lined in pain are soothed beneath the artist's loving hand"?

Confucius @MasterSays
You get me. "Now you understand what I try to say to you."

§ Session 03.08

---

[8] Source text quotes a line from the lyric "Stately Beauty", collected in the *Book of Songs*, Airs of Wèi, No. 3: "What dimpled smile that brings delight / what sultry eyes of black on white!" — a description of the physical beauty of an imperial concubine of Wèi.

[9] Most likely a quote from the Ritual Objects chapter of the *Book of Rites* instructing court artists to apply colors over a blank canvas.

Confucius @MasterSays
I can tell you about the culture of Classical Greece, but don't expect to find it in modern-day Athens; I can tell you about the traditions of Ancient Rome, but don't expect them to be practiced in present-day Italy[10]. These things were never properly passed down, or else we'd see living examples of these magnificent civilizations in our midst.

§ Session 03.09

 **Confucius** is invited to witness an authentic voodoo ritual[11].

Confucius @MasterSays
I'll come to the reception, but won't stay for the part where you behead the chicken.

§ Session 03.10

---

[10] Source text: "I can tell you about the traditions of the Xià, but don't expect to find them in the kingdom of Qǐ (whose rulers are descended from the Xià royal family); I can tell you about the traditions of the Shāng, but don't expect to find them in the kingdom of Sòng (whose rulers are descended from the Shāng royal family)."

[11] Source text references the ritual of imperial ancestral worship known as the "dì". Confucius voices reservations about witnessing portions of the ritual, specifically those that follow the practice of libation.

 **Confucius** is asked about the Rosicrucian Mysteries[12].

Confucius @MasterSays
I wouldn't know. But it is said those initiated into the Order are groomed to become masters of the universe.

§ Session 03.11

Confucius @MasterSays
When you say your daily prayers, pretend as if the angels are listening; when you pray to Almighty God, picture him standing before your eyes. And make sure you do so in person — prayers that are said in your name don't really amount to much.

§ Session 03.12

Joachim Murat @GrandeArmée
They say "Better the devil you know"[13]. Is there any truth to that?

Confucius @MasterSays
Nonsense! If you befriend the devil and incur the wrath of God, all the prayers in the world won't save you.

§ Session 03.13

---

[12] Source text refers to knowledge of the ritual of imperial ancestral worship known as the "dì".

[13] Source text cites the Chinese saying "Better to pray to the Kitchen God than to offer worship to ancestral spirits".

Confucius @MasterSays
The Constitution of the United States[14] is inspired by the Magna Carta and the writings of Enlightenment philosophers such as Thomas Hobbes, Jean-Jacques Rousseau, and John Locke. As constitutions go, this is the jewel in the crown.

§ Session 03.14

 When **Confucius** goes to church[15], he is Mr. Inquisitive, inquiring after every detail of ritual and decorum.

Pastor @ChurchClergy
What is with this guy? Does he have nothing better to do?

Confucius @MasterSays
The Bible teaches, "Only let everything be done in a becoming and orderly manner," does it not?

§ Session 03.15

---

[14] Source text comments on the cultural achievements of the Zhōu, which are built upon the traditions of the Xià and the Shāng but surpass them in sophistication in every way.

[15] Source text refers to the ancestral temple of the royal family of Lǔ.

Confucius @MasterSays
When you win at sports, you don't rub your opponent's nose in the dirt[16]. It's called common courtesy.

§ Session 03.16

Sly @Woodstock
What do you say we put an end to the slaughter of turkeys on Thanksgiving Day?[17]

Confucius @MasterSays
You're sad to see the birds die — I get that, but the alternative is to kill off a venerable American tradition. Now that I cannot live with.

§ Session 03.17

Confucius @MasterSays
I'm just doing my job, but everyone thinks I'm sucking up to the boss.

§ Session 03.18

---

[16] In the source text Confucius harks back on long lost traditions of archery which emphasize marksmanship rather than brute force.

[17] In the source text, Zǐgòng (a.k.a. **Sly** @Woodstock) wishes to do away with the sacrificial lamb at the Ceremony of the New Moon.

King Frederick @SleepyHead
As commander-in-chief, my wish is your command. I give the orders, you follow them. Do I not make myself clear enough?[18]

Confucius @MasterSays
Thomas Carlyle said it well, "Woe to him that claims obedience when it is not due; woe to him that refuses it when it is".

§ Session 03.19

Confucius @MasterSays
If ever there is a voice that is sad but not somber, if ever there is music that is erotic but not obscene, it is Madonna[19].

§ Session 03.20

---

[18] Source text quotes the comments of King Dìng of Lǔ: "A ruler commands his subject; a subject serves his ruler," which is modified by Confucius to "When a ruler commands his subject to do what is proper, the subject serves his ruler with utmost loyalty."

[19] In the source text, Confucius refers to the opening ballad of the Airs of the States "Cry of the Ospreys", collected in the *Book of Songs*.

King Maximilian asks about the pagan origins of the Christmas tree.

Butch @Self
The Picts were partial to the scent of pine; the Romans observed solstice with sprigs of spruce. The Georgians believed candle-lit "firs" could conquer the "fears" of long winter nights[20].

Confucius @MasterSays
Tradition. It is what it is. No point in trying to make sense of it all.

§ Session 03.21

Confucius @MasterSays
To hell with Alexander Haig[21] — the man has no morals!

Interlocuter @Anonymous
Surely he has proven himself on the battlefield.

---

[20] When asked by King Āi of Lǔ about the choice of wood for ancestral altars, Zǎi Wǒ replies that pine was used by the Xià (2207-1766 B.C.), cypress was used by the Shāng (1765-1122 B.C.), while the current Zhōu dynasty (1121-249 B.C.) is inclined to use chestnut (lì), whose name is homophonous with the word for "tremble" (zhànlì).

[21] In this passage, Confucius comments that Guǎn Zhòng, famed minister of the state of Qí, was neither frugal nor knowledgeable in matters of protocol. He was less than frugal because he maintained three residences with dedicated staff; he was deemed ignorant of protocol (or willfully disregardful of it) because he usurped practices normally reserved for the emperor, such as using boxwood to accentuate private entrances and providing bar carts at private functions.

Confucius @MasterSays
How many four-star generals do you know who have never achieved the rank of lieutenant general, who just sit their asses in Washington all day and bully their way to the top?

Interlocuter @ Anonymous
But some say he's fiercely loyal to his country.

Confucius @MasterSays
Loyal my ass! As Nixon's Chief-of-Staff, he ran a spy ring around the White House that brought down the presidency. And when Reagan was shot in 81, he wasted no time in announcing he was in control, despite the Constitution saying otherwise. If that can be called loyal, there isn't a traitor in Hell who doesn't deserve a Purple Heart.

§ Session 03.22

 Confucius explains to the new lounge pianist how to play Beethoven's "Moonlight Sonata"[22].

Confucius @MasterSays
Playing this piece isn't hard, really. You start out slow with an adagio sostenuto, then pick up the pace as you transition to allegretto, and finally, you have a stormy presto agigato, replete with multiple arpeggios, to bring the music to a climax.

§ Session 03.23

 An airport immigration official[23] asks Confucius to step aside.

Airport Security @LAX
Pope or president, everyone goes through me.

 The official emerges after the interview and speaks to Confucius's entourage.

Airport Security @LAX
Cheer up, you guys! Why bemoan the state of the world? We've already hit rock bottom — the only way to go is up. This guy here is our savior!

§ Session 03.24

---

[22] In the source text, Confucius explains to musicians of the Lǔ court the styles of the different movements of traditional court music.

[23] Source text describes a border guard at the crossing point of Yí (situated in the state of Wèi) asking to speak with Confucius.

Commenting on **Beethoven**'s "Ode to Joy".

Confucius @MasterSays
Aesthetically perfect and morally inspiring.

Commenting on **Coolio**'s "Gangsta's Paradise".

Confucius @MasterSays
Aesthetically appealing but morally corrupting.

§ Session 03.25

Confucius @MasterSays
When you have someone who is ruthless in power, who treats the system like a joke and shows no respect in times of mourning, I'm not sure how I can take somebody like that seriously.

§ Session 03.26

40

COMMUNITY

里仁

Confucius @MasterSays
Move to a good neighborhood. Live in the ghetto? That can't be smart.

§ Session 04.01

Confucius @MasterSays
They crash and burn when money is flush; they scam and steal when times are lean. That's your typical lowlife, unlike his more congenial counterpart, who is content to live a charitable life, or his more intelligent counterpart, who knows that it pays to be nice.

§ Session 04.02

Confucius @MasterSays
Be sure you're perfect before you go around judging other people.

§ Session 04.03

Confucius @MasterSays
If you have the heart to do good, you can't be all that bad.

§ Session 04.04

Confucius @MasterSays
Like every other man, I'm attracted to wealth and status, but not when acquired through dubious means. Like every kid from the projects, I dream of escaping poverty and squalor, but not if it means compromising my principles. Without my principles, I'm nothing. Which is why, come hell or high water, I'll always hold fast to my principles.

§ Session 04.05

Confucius @MasterSays
I've yet to see anyone truly abhor evil or hold fast to what is good. Those who hold fast to what is good naturally leave little to be desired; those who abhor evil are followers of good in the sense that they strive to keep evil at arm's length. If only we could get people to devote but a single day to the pursuit of good, what a world of difference it would make. Just one day — but I've yet to see anyone capable of it. That's not to say there aren't such people, just that I haven't met any.

§ Session 04.06

 **Confucius** @MasterSays
I'm only human,
Of flesh and blood I'm made;
I'm only human,
Born to make mistakes.

Our mistakes speak volumes about who we are — they are, in essence, what makes us human.

§ Session 04.07

 **Confucius** @MasterSays
Let the truth be heard, even if it means I won't live to see the light of day.

§ Session 04.08

 **Confucius** @MasterSays
If you claim the moral high ground but can't stand to starve or sleep rough, what kind of moral crusader are you anyway?

§ Session 04.09

 **Confucius** @MasterSays
To a man of the world, there is no absolute right or wrong. The truth depends on the circumstances.

§ Session 04.10

Confucius @MasterSays
There are those who are guided by higher principles, and there are those who seek out more earthly pleasures. There are those who live for the present moment, and there are those who live for posterity.

§ Session 04.11

Confucius @MasterSays
If you're only asking "What's in it for me?", you're going to see a lot of unhappy people.

§ Session 04.12

Confucius @MasterSays
If mighty nations are founded on civility and tolerance, who wouldn't want to embrace these values? If the major powers do not embrace civility and tolerance, what good is civil society anyway?

§ Session 04.13

Confucius @MasterSays
Don't ask why you're out of a job, ask why you're deserving of one. Don't say you don't know the right people — make the right people want to get to know you.

§ Session 04.14

Confucius @MasterSays
You know, in the end, it all comes down to one tiny little thing.

Jonathan @JonoSays
I hear you.

Upon the master's departure, the disciples swarm **Jonathan**.

Interlocuter @Anonymous
What's he talking about?

Jonathan @JonoSays
It's all about empathy, stupid. All you need is love.

§ Session 04.15

Confucius @MasterSays
There are those moved by a sense of moral obligation, and then there are those lured by the scent of money.

§ Session 04.16

Confucius @MasterSays
Good role models inspire you to greatness; bad role models show you what can go wrong.

§ Session 04.17

Confucius @MasterSays
With your parents, be kind but firm.
Speak up with the understanding that
they may not take it very well. But keep
your displeasure to yourself.

§ Session 04.18

Confucius @MasterSays
Don't go wandering off without telling
your parents where you'll be and when
you'll be back.

§ Session 04.19

Confucius @MasterSays
A good son is one who takes over the
family business, and, three years on, out
of respect for the father, has no intention
whatsoever of changing the way things
are run.

§ Session 04.20

Confucius @MasterSays
Make a note of your parents' age, for in
their advanced years you'll find cause for
celebration and cause for concern.

§ Session 04.21

Confucius @MasterSays
In the olden days, people said much less because their words counted for much more.

§ Session 04.22

Confucius @MasterSays
When in doubt, keep a low profile.

§ Session 04.23

Confucius @MasterSays
People ought to be small on talk and big on action.

§ Session 04.24

Confucius @MasterSays
When you take the moral high ground, you won't be standing alone.

§ Session 04.25

Yanni @Yannopolous
Try too hard and you'll get on people's nerves. Come on too hard and you'll scare your prospects away.

§ Session 04.26

COURTSHIP

公冶長

Commenting on **Jailbird John.**

Confucius @MasterSays
He'd make a good son-in-law. He's fresh out of prison, but he was serving time for crimes he did not commit.

 **Confucius** gives **John** his daughter's hand in marriage.

§ Session 05.01

Commenting on **Dixie Chet.**

Confucius @MasterSays
In good times, he'll find ways to make himself useful; in bad times, he'll know to stay out of trouble.

 **Confucius** gives **Chet** his niece's hand in marriage.

§ Session 05.02

Commenting on **Matthew McConaughey.**

Confucius @MasterSays
What a classy, all-American sweetheart! Don't tell me they don't raise them like that anymore, because if so, how'd he learn to be such a southern gentleman?[1]

§ Session 05.03

---

[1] Confucius says of his disciple Mì Zǐjiàn, "What a man of character! They say there are no real men left in the Kingdom of Lǔ. But if so, who raised him to be the man that he is?"

Sly @Woodstock
What do I remind you of?

Confucius @MasterSays
You're like one of those fixtures in a stately home.

Sly @Woodstock
Yeah? What kind of fixture?

Confucius @MasterSays
A white elephant[2].

§ Session 05.04

They say of **Roland** that he's a great guy, just a bit quiet.

Confucius @MasterSays
What's wrong with being quiet? It's the talkative ones who usually get into trouble. Whether Roland's a great guy I don't know, but what's wrong with being quiet?

§ Session 05.05

---

[2] Source text compares Zǐgòng (a.k.a. **Sly** @Woodstock) to a ritual vessel "húlián" used for storing grains, the metaphorical significance of which has been obscured with time.

▶▶ **Confucius** recommends **Chad** for a government post.

Chad @Carver
Not sure I'm up to it, teach.

▶▶ Hearing this, **Confucius** is secretly pleased.

§ Session 05.06

Confucius @MasterSays
When the world comes to an end and the only human survivors are adrift on an ark, I expect I would find you there with me, Louie.

Louie appears pleased.

Confucius @MasterSays
Why Louie, when it comes to daring, you are many times the man that I am, only you must learn to rein in your impulses.

§ Session 05.07

Rodrigo de Borgia @AlexanderVI
Is Louie a good person deep down?

Confucius @MasterSays
Hard to say.

Rodrigo de Borgia @AlexanderVI
What do you mean?

Confucius @MasterSays
Put him at the head of the imperial army
and he'd make a darn fine commander.
But as to whether he is good deep down,
I really don't know.

Rodrigo de Borgia @AlexanderVI
What about Randall? Is he a good
person deep down?

Confucius @MasterSays
Put him at the head of a prosperous
state or a decent-size city, and he'd
make a popular mayor or governor. But
whether he is a good person deep down,
I really cannot tell.

Rodrigo de Borgia @AlexanderVI
What about Florian? Is he good deep
down?

Confucius @MasterSays
Florian is well-spoken and has an
amazing sense of style. He would make
the perfect ambassador. But as for
whether he is good deep down, your
guess is as good as mine.

§ Session 05.08

Confucius @MasterSays
So, how do you stack up against Owen?

Sly @Woodstock
Owen? You've got to be kidding. I mean, some people might say I'm ahead of the curve, but Owen, he is in a league of his own.

Confucius @MasterSays
That makes two of us who feel this way.

§ Session 05.09

Butch is caught dozing off in broad daylight.

Confucius @MasterSays
You don't cook omelettes with rotten eggs; you can't make salad out of chicken shit[3]. That's what you are, Butch, rotten to the core, a useless piece of shit. What am I supposed to do with you? You know, I used to give people the benefit of the doubt, but now I don't believe it until I see it. It is you, Butch, who has made a cynic out of me.

§ Session 05.10

---

[3] Source text: "You can't create sculptures out of rotting wood; you can't plaster over a wall of manure."

Confucius @MasterSays
You're lacking in strength of character, every one of you.

Interlocuter @Anonymous
Even Romeo Montecchio?[4]

Confucius @MasterSays
"Romeo and Juliet" Romeo? Why, he's so weighed down by desire, what strength is there left to spare?

§ Session 05.11

Sly @Woodstock
I wouldn't do to others what I don't want others to do to me.

Confucius @MasterSays
Nice thought, Sly, but I'm not quite sure you're there yet.

§ Session 05.12

---

[4] In the source text the unnamed interlocutor gives the example of Confucian disciple Shēn Chéng, known for his attachment to dogma, as an example of strength and conviction, only to be refuted by Confucius, who explains that obsession is not the same as strength.

Sly @Woodstock
We're all familiar with the master's scholarly prowess, but it is his private thoughts on God and the human condition, known only to a select few, that I find the most fascinating.

§ Session 05.13

 **Louie** resents being swamped with new details before he is able to process the information at hand.

§ Session 05.14

Sly @Woodstock
Why was dunk legend Julius Erving of the Philadelphia 76ers called "Doctor J"?[5]

Confucius @MasterSays
He had planned on becoming a doctor, though he never finished college. But thanks to his achievements on the basketball court, he was awarded an honorary doctorate by his alma mater.

§ Session 05.15

---

[5] Source text: "Why was Kǒng Wénzǐ given the posthumous appellation of "Wén" (cultured, sophisticated) when he was anything but?" Confucius then goes on to explain that at least he tried, extolling the merits of effort.

Confucius @MasterSays
Otto von Bismarck[6] was in every way a statesman par excellence: he carried himself with dignity and held the Kaiser in the highest regard; he treated his people generously and steered the populace towards worthy causes.

§ Session 05.16

Confucius @MasterSays
Thomas Jefferson[7] was a master of diplomacy. After a while, you cannot but marvel at his abilities.

§ Session 05.17

Confucius @MasterSays
The outsize country estate of Ukrainian president Viktor Yanukovych features a private zoo as well as tubs and toilets plated with gold[8]. The man is way in over his head.

§ Session 05.18

---

[6] In the source text, Confucius praises the virtues of Zǐchǎn (a.k.a. Gōngsūn Qiáo), minister of the state of Zhèng.

[7] In the source text, Confucius marvels at the diplomatic prowess of Yàn Píngzhòng, minister of the state of Qí.

[8] In the source text, Confucius questions the judgment of Lǔ minister Zāng Wénzhòng (a.k.a. Zāngsūn Chén), believed by many to be a man of wisdom. Confucius's criticism is aimed at Zāng's lavish lifestyle, which includes a mansion that houses giant tortoises (for use in divination) and beams and pillars carved in the shape of mountains and reefs — designs reserved for the emperor.

Ezra @Johnson
Grover Cleveland[9] was elected to the presidency three times and oversaw two transitions of power. In his moments of victory there was no euphoria, and when forced to relinquish control he was anything but wistful. Each time he would dutifully brief his successor and facilitate transition to the next administration. What do you make of a man like this?

Confucius @MasterSays
He is dutiful to be sure.

Ezra @Johnson
Would you call him a saint?

Confucius @MasterSays
God, no! In what way is he saintly?

---

[9] In the source text, Zǐzhāng (a.k.a. **Yanni** @Yannopolous) asks about the virtues of legendary Chǔ minister Zǐwén, who was pivotal in improving the fortunes of the southern state of Chǔ.

Ezra @Johnson
When his *Letters Concerning the English Nation* was burned by Louis XV of France, Voltaire[10] fled Paris for Potsdam, where he was welcomed by Frederick the Great of Prussia. When Voltaire's vitriol turned to the Berlin Academy of Science however, it was Frederick who torched his books and called for his arrest, forcing him to seek refuge in Geneva. What do you make of this guy Voltaire?

Confucius @MasterSays
He dares to speak the truth.

Ezra @Johnson
Does that make him a saint?

Confucius @MasterSays
I don't see how that makes him saintly.

§ Session 05.19

---

[10] Source text details how when the sovereign of Qí was assassinated by his minister Cuī Zhù, fellow minister Chén Wénzǐ abandoned his sizeable estate in the kingdom in search of a more deserving ruler to serve under, only to be disappointed time and again, prompting him to comment each time that, "they are no different from the usurper Cuī Zhù".

 **Prince Hamlet** is in the habit of thinking twice and then again before committing to any action[11].

Confucius @MasterSays
Twice is plenty enough.

§ Session 05.20

Confucius @MasterSays
The genius of David[12] is that in his brightest hour he is king among men, and yet in his darker moments he knows to play the fool. Now history has no shortage of able kings, but how many can actually hunker down and play the fool?

§ Session 05.21

---

[11] In the source text, Confucius's remark is directed at the indecisiveness of Lǔ minister Jì Wénzǐ.

[12] Source text praises Wèi minister Níng Wǔzǐ for his ability to play dumb when forces conspire against him.

 On a pilgrimage to the land of milk and honey[13].

Confucius @MasterSays
Time to go back. Time to go back to my little ones, so full of promise, so brimming with talent, yet so naively optimistic about fame and glory. They could really use a reality check to temper their high hopes.

§ Session 05.22

Confucius @MasterSays
Paul and Peter[14] practiced forgiveness, and in turn, were given the benefit of the doubt.

§ Session 05.23

---

[13] Confucius visits the kingdom of Chén.

[14] Source text makes reference to the Shāng princes Bó Yí and Shú Qí, known for their moral aptitude and pacifist tendencies, who chose to starve to death rather than aid in the Zhōu clan's rebellion against the Shāng dynasty.

Confucius @MasterSays
They say Michael Jackson[15] was quite the philanthropist, over time donating millions to charities around the world. But what with his bankruptcy later in life, you could argue he was just robbing Peter to pay Paul.

§ Session 05.24

Confucius @MasterSays
Boccaccio[16] didn't stand for panderers who go out of their way to please and neither do I. Boccaccio didn't care for hypocrites who put on a friendly face for those they despise and neither do I.

§ Session 05.25

---

[15] Source text refers to Wēishēng Gāo, a citizen of Lǔ known for being charitable. Not much else is known about the man.

[16] Source text refers to famed historian Zuǒ Qiūmíng (502-422 B.C.), author of the *Zuǒ Commentary* on the *Spring and Autumn Annals*.

 Confucius sits with **Louie** and **Owen** at his side.

Confucius @MasterSays
Let's hear your life's ambitions.

Louie @Walker
Cars, toys, and fancy clothes, and I wouldn't bat an eyelid about sharing them with my friends.

Owen @Yentl
Don't want to bring attention to myself, and don't want to inconvenience other people.

Louie @Walker
And you, master?

Confucius @MasterSays
I'd like for my elders to approve of me, for my peers to know they can count on me, and for my little ones to look to me for comfort and protection[17].

§ Session 05.26

---

[17] Coming from glaringly different socioeconomic backgrounds, **Louie** @Walker is driven to impress his peers, whereas **Owen** @Yentl is preoccupied with caring for the elderly. In formulating his own reply, Confucius acknowledges the need for both types of aspirations, but adds to the list the nurturing of the young, which fittingly encapsulates his relationship with both **Louie** and **Owen**.

Confucius @MasterSays
To hell with it! I've yet to meet anyone who is aware of his own shortcomings and is working to overcome them.

§ Session 05.27

Confucius @MasterSays
I'll bet you can find reliable people like me in every little town across the country. The question is, are they as inquisitive as I am?

§ Session 05.28

PROTÉGÉS

Roland inquires after **Diogenes of Sinope**[1].

Confucius @MasterSays
He's a laid back, go easy kind of guy.

Roland @Archer
You'd think you'd want to go hard on yourself but go easy on others if you want to command some respect. If you're easy on yourself and easy on others, what can you ever hope to accomplish?

Confucius @MasterSays
You got a point there. Why, Roland, someday you're going to make a name for yourself.

§ Session 06.01

---

[1] In the source text, the conversation centers around the virtues of one Zǐsāng Bózǐ, of which little is known. A more detailed account of Confucius's encounter with Zǐsāng Bózǐ appears in the Hàn dynasty story collection *Shuō Yuan*, according to which Zǐsāng Bózǐ shows up in the nude when Confucius comes calling at his door, raising the eyebrows of many in Confucius's party, who ask the master why he would bother to call on such a wild man. Confucius answers that Zǐsāng is good deep down, and that the encounter hopefully would encourage Zisāng to adopt more civilized ways. The followers of Zǐsāng Bózǐ, meanwhile, ask their mentor why he would bother to meet with someone as pompous as Confucius, to which Zǐsāng replies that Confucius is a good person deep down, and that the encounter hopefully would encourage Confucius to abandon his extravagant pretentions and live life closer to nature. We interpolate the commentary with *Shuō Yuan*'s account of the meeting in Session 06.02.

 **Confucius** pays a visit to **Diogenes of Sinope**, who greets his house guest in the buff. Disciples of Confucius ask why he would bother to call on such a wild man.

 **Confucius** @MasterSays
He's a good person deep down. By meeting with him, I'm hoping to get him to adopt more civilized ways.

 Following the encounter, disciples of **Diogenes of Sinope** ask why their master would bother to entertain one as pompous as **Confucius**.

Diogenes @Sinope
He's a good person deep down. By meeting with him, I'm hoping to get him to abandon his pretensions and live life closer to nature.

§ Session 06.02

 **King Maximilian** @LastKnight
Who among your students would you consider exceptional?

Confucius @MasterSays
Exceptional I would only use on Owen, who never raises his voice and seldom repeats a mistake. But Owen, may he rest in peace, is no longer of this world. As for the ones who are, I wouldn't call any of them exceptional.

§ Session 06.03

 **Florian** is dispatched as ambassador to Britain, leaving behind his elderly mother, for whom **Randall** seeks a monthly stipend[2].

Confucius @MasterSays
A few hundred should cover it.

Randall @RandSays
You've got to do better than that.

Confucius @MasterSays
I'll go as far as a grand.

 **Randall** ends up giving her four grand a month.

Confucius @MasterSays
From what I remember, Florian wasn't exactly scrimping by, flying first class to London, dressed from head to toe in the latest fashions. We're in the business of giving benefits to the needy, not supplementing the lifestyles of the rich.

§ Session 06.04

---

[2] Source text describes how when Confucian disciple Zǐhuá (a.k.a. **Florian** @Westwood) is dispatched to the kingdom of Qí, the negotiated amount of rations for Zǐhuá's aging mother go from a two week allowance to a five week allowance, eventually ballooning to an excessive thirty week allowance of grains.

 As chaplain of the Royal Household, **Shane** is given a stipend of $9,000[3], which he refuses out of principle.

Confucius @MasterSays
Come on, take it, if not for yourself, for the needy folks back home.

§ Session 06.05

Speaking to **Roland**.

Confucius @MasterSays
When the offspring of a motley dairy cow sports fifty-inch horns and grows to be two thousand pounds of pure darkness, what are the chances he'll be grazing on a pasture in Guernsey instead of fighting in a bull ring in Pamplona?[4]

§ Session 06.06

Confucius @MasterSays
Only Owen can see no evil and hear no evil; the rest of us are lucky to make it through the day.

§ Session 06.07

---

[3] Yuán Sī is given nine hundred measures of grain, a large amount by the standards of the day.

[4] Source text: "When the offspring of a motley cow sports the dark red coat and straight pointed horns of a sacrificial ox, even if you were loathe to offer him up for sacrifice, do you think the God of the Mountains and Rivers would allow you to keep him to yourself?"

Cosimo de Medici @ilGrande
Would Louie make a good leader?

Confucius @MasterSays
Louie is a man of action. I see little that can stand in his way.

Cosimo de Medici @ilGrande
What about Sly?

Confucius @MasterSays
Sly is highly intelligent, and can see to the bottom of any problem.

Cosimo de Medici @ilGrande
And Randall?

Confucius @MasterSays
Randall is immensely talented. His talent will carry him through.

§ Session 06.08

Donald Trump names **Mason** to serve as director of the FBI[5].

Mason @Withers
With all due respect, I decline. And if I'm presented with other similar offers, I'd sooner emigrate to Canada.

§ Session 06.09

---

[5] The unscrupulous Jì clan wishes for Mǐn Zǐqiān (a.k.a. **Mason** @Withers) to be steward of their Bì family estate, to which Mǐn replies, "Say no to them nicely. And if they ask again, I'll have no choice but to hide out north of the Wèn river (i.e., move to a different country)."

Rhett is rushed to the ER. **Confucius** stands at his bedside holding his hand.

Confucius @MasterSays
We're going to lose him, and there's nothing the doctors can do. To think, a misfortune like this striking a good man like that. Unbelievable! Unbelievable!

§ Session 06.10

Confucius @MasterSays
What a man, this Owen, living on the street, not knowing where his next meal is coming from. People worry for his health, yet he simply revels in life's simple pleasures. What a man!

§ Session 06.11

Randall @Randsays
It's not that I don't want to learn from you, but that I'm just not cut out for it.

Confucius @MasterSays
Those who aren't cut out for it would have given up long ago. With you, it's more like you're drawing a line and refusing to cross it.

§ Session 06.12

Speaking to **Auguste**.

Confucius @MasterSays
Be an impartial scholar; don't be a petty academic.

§ Session 06.13

 Newly nominated to White House Chief-of-Staff, **Yanni** is busy filling cabinet vacancies.

Confucius @MasterSays
Any promising new hopefuls?

Yanni @Yannopolous
Well, there is this Sheldon Cooper[6] character, who doesn't cut corners and never mixes business with pleasure.

§ Session 06.14

---

[6] When asked by Confucius whether he had discovered any promising new talent after being appointed governor of Wǔchéng (a territory in Confucius's home state of Lǔ), Zǐyóu singles out a staff member by the name of Tántái Mièmíng, who "does not take shortcuts and does not enter the governor's mansion for anything other than official business". Tántái Mièmíng later becomes a disciple of Confucius.

Confucius @MasterSays
General Robert E. Lee[7] is not one for grandstanding. Upon his defeat at Gettysburg, he writes, "no one is more aware than myself of my inability for the duties of my position". Prior to his surrender to the Union Army, he sighs, "I would rather die a thousand deaths."

§ Session 06.15

Confucius @MasterSays
In this age, to be blessed with the looks of a Mark Wahlberg but not with the brains of a Mark Zuckerberg is to be consigned to a life of frustration[8].

§ Session 06.16

---

[7] Source text: "General Mèng Zhifǎn was not given to bragging about his achievements. He led the rear guard at the ambush of Jìqū, and when his routed forces finally made it home, he explained it wasn't his courage that led him to serve as a buffer against the encroaching enemy, but the fact that his horse was slow."

[8] Source text makes reference to the good looks of Sòng Zhāo (an aristocrat from the state of Sòng known for his way with women) and the eloquence of Zhù Tuó (a minister of the state of Wèi known for his way with words).

Confucius @MasterSays
Look, there's no way out of this room
except through that door; there's no way
to a better future than down the straight
and narrow path.

§ Session 06.17

Confucius @MasterSays
Show more candor than sophistication
and you risk being labeled a fool; let your
sophistication outweigh your candor, and
people will call you pretentious. Aim for a
balance between the two.

§ Session 06.18

Confucius @MasterSays
The good sail through life with few cares
or doubts; the wicked are constantly
looking over their shoulders.

§ Session 06.19

Confucius @MasterSays
Better to be an aficionado than a
connoisseur; better to be a connoisseur
than a dilettante.

§ Session 06.20

Confucius @MasterSays
Speak of God only to those with above average intelligence; do not broach the subject with those who are sub par.

§ Session 06.21

Francis asks how to do the smart thing.

Confucius @MasterSays
Do right by your people and kiss up to the powers that be so they don't meddle in your affairs. That's what I call smart.

Francis asks how to do the right thing.

Confucius @MasterSays
Put in the hard work first and *then* expect results. That would be the right thing to do.

§ Session 06.22

Confucius @MasterSays
The wise are mercurial like water; the good are earthy as the rolling hills. The wise are on the move; the good remain in place. The wise seek out thrills; the good play it safe[9].

§ Session 06.23

Confucius @MasterSays
With due changes, Mexico can become more like America. With due changes, America can become Pax Romana[10].

§ Session 06.24

---

[9] Modern scholars have interpreted this dichotomy as a study in contrasts between the conservative values of Confucius's native state of Lǔ and the more liberal views of its stronger and more prosperous neighbor Qí, both situated in present-day Shāndōng province. Whereas Lǔ is landlocked and subsists on agriculture, Qí enjoys long coastlines and thrives on trade, resulting in a more tolerant and open society that values cultural admixture and intellectual exchange, in contrast to the more inward-looking world view of Lǔ, which places greater emphasis on nobility and ancient traditions inherited from the Zhōu.

[10] Source text: "With due changes, the state of Qí could be more like the state of Lǔ; with due changes, the state of Lǔ could be more in touch with the Way of Heaven (the 'Tao')."

Confucius @MasterSays
If a champagne isn't produced in Champagne-Ardenne, is it still a champagne? Is it really champagne?[11]
§ Session 06.25

Butch @Self
Look at those angry picketers casting holier-than-thou glances! You think if I tell them there was a drowning seal pup at the bottom of that oil well, they'd all jump to their deaths and go to hell?[12]

Confucius @MasterSays
Now, come on, why would they do such a thing? They're activists, not airheads. You can play on their sympathy, but you can't take away their good sense. You can mislead them, but you'll never outwit them.
§ Session 06.26

---

[11] Source text presents a commentary on the bronze age ritual drinking vessel known as the *gū*, which in the Shāng dynasty was made to exacting standards, but by Confucius's time had grown in size and lost its original form thanks to the later penchant for excessive drinking, to which Confucius asks, "If the *gū* no longer resembles a *gū*, is it still a *gū*?", which scholars have interpreted variably as a lament for the loss of ritual propriety or as a criticism of the alcoholic excesses of late Zhōu society.

[12] Source text: "With (self-) righteous people, if you were to tell them 'goodness lies at the bottom of that well,' would they all rush to jump in?"

Confucius @MasterSays
You'd be surprised how far an education and some coaching in etiquette would get you in life.

§ Session 06.27

 In advance of his visit to the Trump White House, **Confucius** meets with **Ivanka** at Mar-a-Lago[13]. **Louie** is displeased.

Confucius @MasterSays
God be my witness if I have done anything wrong.

§ Session 06.28

Confucius @MasterSays
All things in moderation — that is the key to everything. A shame few people can stick to such a regimen!

§ Session 06.29

---

[13] Prior to his audience with King Líng of Wèi, Confucius meets with the king's consort Nánzǐ, who oversteps her authority in demanding that all visiting dignitaries be vetted by her.

Sly @Woodstock
Say you have a head of state who distributes wealth equitably and provides relief when disaster strikes. Would you call him a good leader?[14]

Confucius @MasterSays
A good leader indeed — why, the man is practically a saint, for even the Dalai Lama and the Holy Father fall short on this measure[15]. You see, a good leader is one who helps others prosper where he has prospered, and pushes them to succeed where he has succeeded. Spread the love — that's the way to go!

§ Session 06.30

---

[14] Source text asks whether a person who meets these criteria is worthy of the label *rén*, i.e., "empathetic" or "humane".

[15] Source text: "Even the mythical emperors Yáo and Shùn fall short on this measure."

TRADITION

述而

Confucius @MasterSays
Some call me an intellectual cowboy[1],
Some say I'm a philosopher for the ages;
Some people call me Socrates,
Cuz I recount the teachings of the sages,
Cuz I'm traditional, I'm unoriginal,
I don't bring to the table anything
additional.

§ Session 07.01

Confucius @MasterSays
All my life I've been a quiet observer, a
committed learner, and a devoted
teacher. How hard can that be, really?

§ Session 07.02

Confucius @MasterSays
My fears are that my morals would elude
me and my work ethic would desert me,
or that I would witness injustice and not
have the power to act, or see personal
weakness and not be open to change.
These worries are constantly on my
mind.

§ Session 07.03

In his spare time, **Confucius** is laid back and
relaxed.

§ Session 07.04

---

[1] Source text: "I pass on the old and contribute nothing new; I have
absolute faith in the traditions of the ancients — why, I'd like to think I'm
the modern day incarnation of the mythical sage Péng Zǔ."

Confucius @MasterSays
I must be losing it, for it's been an eternity since the archangel Gabriel[2] last appeared in my dreams.

§ Session 07.05

Confucius @MasterSays
Commit to a greater cause. Follow your moral compass, listen to your conscience, and immerse yourself in noble pursuits.

§ Session 07.06

Confucius @MasterSays
I've yet to turn away any student who shows up at my door with a brown bag and a curious mind[3].

§ Session 07.07

---

[2] Source text speaks of the Duke of Zhōu (known for his interpretation of dreams) no longer appearing to Confucius in his dreams.

[3] Source text gives "any student who shows up with a bundle of cured meats", which has been subject to different interpretations: some treat the cured meats as the standard tuition of the day, which implies Confucius teaches anyone who pays up (regardless of social standing); others see the cured meats as a particularly meager form of payment, suggesting that Confucius teaches even those from the most humble backgrounds.

Explaining his philosophy of teaching.

Confucius @MasterSays
Don't offer any help unless they're hopelessly lost; don't give any hints until they're at their wits' end. And after receiving clues if they still can't put two and two together, then it's a lost cause.

§ Session 07.08

 When at a funeral reception, **Confucius** makes a point not to stuff himself.

§ Session 07.09

 When the crowd starts to get all teary-eyed, he removes his wireless headset[4].

§ Session 07.10

---

[4] Source text: "On such a day (i.e., the day of the funeral) Confucius is moved to tears and resists the urge to break into song."

Confucius @MasterSays
You and I, we're the only ones who know to give it our all when our talents are appreciated, and to take our business elsewhere when they are not.

Louie @Walker
Oh, yeah? Consider this. If you were commander of an army going to war, who would you rather have at your side?

Confucius @MasterSays
Definitely not the sky-diving, alligator-wrestling type[5]. Better to have someone who fears for his life and strategizes to get out on top.

§ Session 07.11

---

[5] Source text has "not the type to fight a tiger with his bare hands or cross a raging river on foot (i.e., the type with nothing to lose)". The tiger-fighting, river-crossing metaphor is borrowed from the lyric "Heaven's Ire" from the *Book of Songs*, Minor Odes, Fifth Decade, No. 1.

Confucius @MasterSays
If I had the chance to make big money, I'd go for it even if it meant I had to work as a bouncer outside some seedy nightclub[6]. But if it isn't meant to be, then I'd rather just spend my time doing the things I love.

§ Session 07.12

Confucius @MasterSays
Life demands absolute sobriety in the face of three things: worship, war, and disease.

§ Session 07.13

After seeing the Grateful Dead live in concert, **Confucius**, for months on end, wanted nothing to do with the creature comforts of his pampered existence[7].

Confucius @MasterSays
Who would have thought music could do this to a person.

§ Session 07.14

---

[6] Source text has "a coachman carrying a whip".

[7] Source text describes how, after having been in the presence of the heavenly Sháo music of the Qí court, earthly delicacies such as cooked meat hold little appeal.

Randall @RandSays
You think the master would agree to serve on the president's advisory board?

Sly @Woodstock
Who knows. I'll go ask.

Speaking to **Confucius**.

Sly @Woodstock
What do you make of Elon Musk?[8]

Confucius @MasterSays
He's a visionary businessman and engineer.

Sly @Woodstock
Do you think he regrets quitting the president's business advisory council?

Confucius @MasterSays
What's there to regret? He believes that climate change is real; the president does not. There's not much more he can do if he stays.

---

[8] While touring the state of Wèi under the auspices of the newly installed King Chū, Confucius is asked whether he would support King Chū in his succession battle with his father King Zhuāng. King Zhuāng (bastard son of King Líng) had been banished from the kingdom after a failed attempt at assassinating the influential consort Nánzǐ (see Session 06.28), queen to his father King Líng of Wèi (see Sessions 14.20 and 15.01). Upon King Líng's death in 493 B.C., the king's grandson King Chū succeeded the throne, from whom the exiled King Zhuāng (father of King Chū) sought to wrest power. When asked to comment on the state of affairs, Confucius gives the example of the Shāng dynasty princes Bó Yí and Shú Qí, who, in contrast to the dueling fathers and sons of Wèi, each voluntarily gave up their right to succession.

Returning to **Randall**.

Sly @Woodstock
Yeah, I don't think he'll be joining the board of advisers.

§ Session 07.15

Confucius @MasterSays
There is a distinct pleasure in living on morsels and sleeping rough — better than scrounging off wealth acquired through dubious means, which, to me, is as alien as sipping stardust from a distant galaxy.

§ Session 07.16

Confucius @MasterSays
Give me a few more years to live so that by fifty I may master the Kabbalah[9], and thereafter live life free of regrets.

§ Session 07.17

Confucius is known to lose his southern accent when he lectures in the classroom, when he attends public functions, and when he speaks before a media audience[10].

§ Session 07.18

---

[9] In the source text Confucius asks to extend his mortal life so that he may have the chance to study the *I-Ching* (a.k.a. *Book of Changes*).

[10] Source text: "Confucius switches to 'elegant speech' when he is reciting poetry, lecturing on history, or performing ceremonial rites." Linguists take this passage to be a clue to the diglossic nature of late Zhōu society, whereby in addition to the local vernacular, an official language of the imperial court is used by educated speakers in more formal situations.

 **Ole McCoy**[11] inquires after **Confucius**, to which **Louie** offers no comment.

 **Confucius** @MasterSays
Next time you ought to answer, "He is the type to skip a meal when lost in a book, who would forget his sorrows in a moment of joy, and who is scarce aware that old age is fast approaching".

§ Session 07.19

 **Confucius** @MasterSays
Don't think for a minute that I was born with the knowledge. I simply have a fascination with the past, and have spent an inordinate amount of time researching civilizations of antiquity.

§ Session 07.20

 **Confucius** isn't the type to marvel over alien abductions, ghost sightings, psychic powers, and other off-the-wall paranoia[12].

§ Session 07.21

---

[11] In the source text Shěn Zhūliáng, county chief of Yè in the southern kingdom of Chǔ, inquires after Confucius from disciple Zǐlù (a.k.a. **Louie** @Walker).

[12] Source text: "Confucius speaks not of malevolent spirits or supernatural forces."

Confucius @MasterSays
Stare at three people in a lineup and certain traits are going to jump out at you. You'll want to acquire the more desirable qualities and lose the mannerisms that paint you as the culprit.

§ Session 07.22

Confucius @MasterSays
God made me the big-hearted man that I am. The Gambinos[13] don't like it? Tough. What are they going to do about it?

§ Session 07.23

Confucius @MasterSays
You think I'm hiding something? You've got to believe me, I'm telling you everything I know. You know me, there isn't a detail of my life that I don't share with the two of you — that's the kind of guy I am.

§ Session 07.24

---

[13] Source text: "What could Huán Tuí possibly do to me?" Huán Tuí, according to Sīmǎ Qiān's *Records of the Grand Historian*, was a military commander who harassed Confucius during one of his lectures and forced the master and his entourage to leave the state of Sòng.

 The four qualities that **Confucius** seeks to bring out in people: dedication, sophistication, credibility, and integrity.

§ Session 07.25

 **Confucius** @MasterSays
I've missed out on the chivalry of knights in armor and have to settle for the hierarchy of the corporate office[14]; I've yet to meet a man who is honest to the bone have to settle for the odd bonehead who can get his story straight, by which I mean not pretending to be that which he is not — not a novice masquerading as an old-timer, a pauper passing for a prince, or an ignoramus purporting to be knowledgeable.

§ Session 07.26

 **Confucius** takes to fishing, but always with a rod, never with a dragnet. He enjoys hunting geese, but shoots only those in flight, never at nesting chicks.

§ Session 07.27

---

[14] In the source text Confucius laments that he has yet to meet an individual worthy of sainthood, but would settle instead for a man of class; he comments also that he has yet to meet a truly good individual, but would settle for one whose character is consistent throughout.

Confucius @MasterSays
No doubt there are geniuses in this world who produce stunning masterpieces without ever having been taught the craft. That's not me. I pore over the works of past masters and heed the comments of noted critics, which is the next best thing after God-given talent, wouldn't you say?

§ Session 07.28

 Confucius allows into the classroom an undocumented student with limited English, which upsets his disciples, who are of the opinion that immigrants from that part of the world are thieves and rapists[15].

Confucius @MasterSays
Don't be so hard on him. Look, the kid wants to learn — shouldn't we be encouraging that? Better to give him an incentive to start afresh than to force him back into his old ways.

§ Session 07.29

Confucius @MasterSays
Who says kindliness is hard to achieve? You have but to want it badly enough, and it is yours.

§ Session 07.30

---

[15] In the source text Confucius is approached by a youth from Hù village, whose inhabitants are notorious for being difficult. Confucius's disciples are surprised that the master is willing to take him in.

>> Judge Judy[16] asks whether the **Duke of Windsor** was noble of character[17].

Confucius @MasterSays
He gave up his throne for the love of his life. It doesn't get any more noble than that!

>> After **Confucius** leaves, **Judge Judy** complains to **Omar**.

Judge Judy @JusticeServed
You'd think he'd know better than to go all giddy over the royals. Edward VIII was a pathetic man-child who saw his affair with the twice-divorced American gold-digger as a cover for his Nazi leanings and sexual inadequacies. To go on record calling her "the woman I love", all the while turning her into a public hate figure, is, to say the least, downright underhanded, don't you think?

---

[16] In the source text, the inquiry is brought about by a judge from the kingdom of Chén.

[17] Source text revolves around the marriage of King Zhāo of Lǔ to the Princess of Wú, both of whom are descended from the Zhōu royal line and share the same family name Jī, between whom marriage is taboo according to local custom. To avoid accusations of incest, the king addresses his bride not by name, but as the firstborn of the king of Wú.

Omar relates **Judge Judy**'s comments to **Confucius**.

Confucius @MasterSays
She called me out, and rightly so. I owe her one.
§ Session 07.31

In a jamming session, **Confucius** lets the lead singer sing solo a second time, then joins in at the refrain.
§ Session 07.32

Confucius @MasterSays
When it comes to teaching and scholarship, I'm about as good as the next person, but if it's personal integrity you're talking about, then, whoa, I still have a long way to go.
§ Session 07.33

Confucius @MasterSays
I am neither saint nor sage, just a dedicated learner and devoted teacher, that's all.

Florian @Westwood
And *that* is where we have some catching up to do.
§ Session 07.34

 Confucius falls ill with **Louie** at his side, who proceeds to offer a prayer.

Confucius @MasterSays
Is that really necessary?

Louie @Walker
Yes, it's necessary. Philippians 4:6: "Don't worry about anything, but in all your prayers ask God for what you need, always asking him with a thankful heart[18]."

Confucius @MasterSays
You don't think that's what I've been doing all along?

§ Session 07.35

Confucius @MasterSays
Wealth begets arrogance, whereas poverty breeds ignorance. If I had to choose between the two, I'd go for ignorance any day.

§ Session 07.36

---

[18] Source text: "As we say in prayer: 'O help me, spirits from above and spirits from below'."

Confucius @MasterSays
Persons of integrity have little to hide, whereas less savory characters harbor deep, dark secrets.

§ Session 07.37

Confucius is mild-mannered yet firm, and commands respect without instilling fear. He appears relaxed and at peace with himself.

§ Session 07.38

EXEMPLARS

泰伯

Confucius @MasterSays
Grover Cleveland[1] was elected to the presidency three times and oversaw two transitions of power. You could not ask for a better exemplar of bipartisan statesmanship.

§ Session 08.01

Confucius @MasterSays
When pushed beyond the bounds of acceptable behavior, graciousness looks like fawning, cautiousness is read as timidity, bravery turns into unruliness, and candor translates to outright tactlessness.

§ Session 08.02

---

[1] Source text praises the selflessness of Prince Tàibó of Zhōu, who thrice yielded the throne to more capable individuals, which worked to the benefit of the people, who are at a loss for words for his generosity.

Confucius @MasterSays
Be true to those who are dear to you if you want others to respond in kind; be supportive of those who stand by you if you don't want others to be ungrateful.

§ Session 08.03

 **Jonathan** awakes from a coma and summons his disciples to his bedside.

Jonathan @JonoSays
See how my hands are shaking? See how my feet are trembling?

As I walk through the valley of the shadow of death,
I take a look at my life and realize there's nothing left[2].

I survived a close one. May this be a lesson to you all.

§ Session 08.04

---

[2] Source text quotes from the lyric "Heaven's Ire" from the *Book of Songs*, Minor Odes, Fifth Decade, No. 1: "With great trepidation / As if on the edge of an abyss / As if treading on thin ice".

 As **Jonathan** clings to life on his deathbed, Cardinal **Alfonso de Borgia** asks if his master has any final wishes.

Jonathan @JonoSays
When a dying swan heaves its final sigh,
It proceeds to sing the sweetest tune;
When a man can sense the end is nigh,
More often than not his words ring true.

Son, are you familiar with the three pillars of civilized behavior?

Alfonso de Borgia @CalixtusIII
Can't say I am.

Jonathan @JonoSays
So indulge me then as I explain it to you one more time. Purity of though protects against vice, purity of action protects against violence, and purity of speech protects against vulgarity. That's all you need to know. As for dress codes and table manners, there are nannies and butlers who can teach it to you — I wouldn't worry too much about it.

§ Session 08.05

Jonathan @JonoSays
Knowledgeable yet deferring to those less learned, capable yet yielding to those less skilled; accomplished yet surprisingly plain-spoken, worldly-wise yet deceptively unassuming — my buddy Owen was that kind of guy.

§ Session 08.06

Jonathan @JonoSays
He who can be trusted with care of the royal heir, who can take charge of a nation of millions, and who, in the most treacherous of circumstances, can stick to his guns is a true man indeed, wouldn't you say?

§ Session 08.07

Jonathan @JonoSays
With a cross on your back and an eternity to go, the journey of the humanist is truly daunting. With the weight of humanity on your back, how can the burden be anything but crushing? With a lifelong commitment to your mission, how can the road ahead not appear endless?

§ Session 08.08

 **Confucius** @MasterSays
Pore over the *Ethics* of Aristotle; relive
Homer's *Odyssey* and fill your ears
with Pythagoras's music of the spheres[3].

§ Session 08.09

Confucius on leadership of a nation.

 **Confucius** @MasterSays
Tell them what to do; no need to tell
them why.

§ Session 08.10

 **Confucius** @MasterSays
When the rich have no regard for the
poor and the suffering becomes
unbearable, society starts to unravel.
When the underclass resorts to violent
tactics, social order starts to break down.

§ Session 08.11

---

[3] Source text: "May the *Book of Songs* inspire you; may the *Book of Rites*
instill character in you; may the *Book of Music* fulfill your deepest needs.

Confucius @MasterSays
You could have the wealth and the stunning looks of a David Beckham and still be reviled by the public if you were found to be an arrogant bastard skimping on child support[4].

§ Session 08.12

Confucius @MasterSays
To graduate from college and not be able to find gainful employment is rare.

§ Session 08.13

Confucius @MasterSays
Have faith in what you were taught and keep doing what is right. Never move to a rogue or terrorist state; don't stay in a country run by fascists. When the world is a just and peaceful place, forge ahead and leave your mark; when it is not, shut your mouth and move along. Shame on you if you're trapped in poverty when most everyone has achieved the American dream; shame on you if you're a billionaire when the 99 percent cannot make ends meet.

§ Session 08.14

---

[4] Source text gives the example of the Duke of Zhōu, known in his day for his talent and his looks.

Confucius @MasterSays
If it's none of your business, stay out of it.

§ Session 08.15

Confucius @MasterSays
"Won't you stay, won't you stay, forever and ever and ever…" Days after listening to Kylie Minogue's "Can't Get You Out of My Head", the tune from the chorus is still ringing in my ears[5].

§ Session 08.16

Confucius @MasterSays
If you're crass yet crafty, stupid yet stubborn, or shallow yet shameless, you are without any redeeming qualities.

§ Session 08.17

---

[5] Source text: "How my ears are still ringing with notes from the climax of *Cry of the Ospreys* played by Chief Musician Zhì."

Confucius @MasterSays
Learning is like chasing after a school bus — if you can't keep up you're going to miss it, or like guarding a pot of gold — if don't look out you're going to lose it[6].

§ Session 08.18

Confucius @MasterSays
How Alexander and Julius Caesar[7] had the world at their fingertips, and yet didn't milk it for all it was worth!

§ Session 08.19

Confucius @MasterSays
Resplendent is David, King of Jews, made after the heart of God Almighty, whose legacy is too vast to name, whose institutions are revered, and whose *Psalms* are a monument for the ages[8].

§ Session 08.20

---

[6] Source text: "Learn as if you can't catch up and are afraid of losing what you have."

[7] Source text praises the leadership styles of Shùn (last of the five mythical emperors) and Yǔ (founder of the Xià dynasty), who were rulers of the known world yet adopted a laid back approach to how things are run.

[8] Source text harks on the legacy of the mythical emperor Yáo, who carried out the will of Heaven with such finesse and to such wondrous effect that his people were in utter awe at his numerous accomplishments.

Confucius @MasterSays
World leaders these days could do with some extra help, wouldn't you say? George Washington had help from the founding fathers; Emmanuel Macron rode to the presidency on the back of his tech team, not to discount the charms of his cougar wife. An army of ministers answers to Angela Merkel, chancellor of Europe's largest economy: to think that Germany accounts for a quarter of European output yet willingly defers to Brussels! What a model of European citizenry![9]

§ Session 08.21

---

[9] Source text comments on how the mythical emperor Shùn was aided by his five able ministers, and how King Wǔ of Zhōu claimed to have had ten men of superior talent at his side, to which Confucius makes the somewhat snide remark that, in truth, there were only nine, because one of them was a woman (believed to be either the King's wife or his mother). Compare with Session 17.25 for a more complete view of the patriarchal nature of Confucian society.

Confucius @MasterSays
Who would have a bad word for FDR, who staved off famine by furnishing school lunches, who restored human dignity by clothing the needy, and who during the housing bubble promoted public works to get the nation back on its feet? Who would have a bad word to say about FDR?[10]

§ Session 08.22

---

[10] In the source text Confucius praises the sound judgment of Xià dynasty founder Yǔ, who spent little on personal luxuries, but spared no expenses when it came to honoring tradition, remembering fallen heroes, and building national infrastructure.

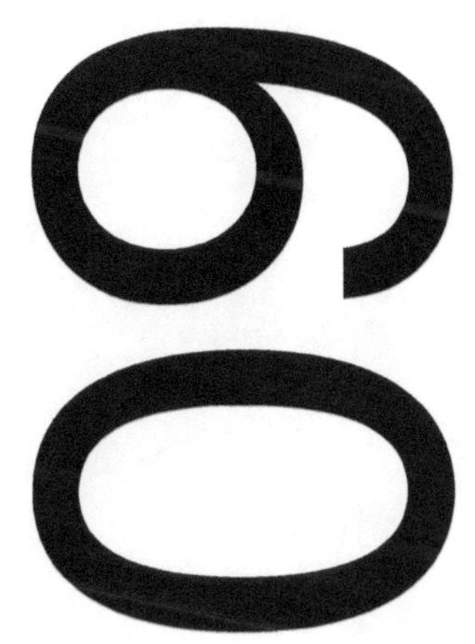

AFTERLIFE

子罕

 **Sergey Brin** believes company profits to be tied to brand image and corporate social responsibility[1].

§ Session 09.01

 **Commentator** @FoxNFriends[2]
Is there nothing that this self-proclaimed "master" does not profess to know? Seems to me like he's a jack of all trades but really a master of none.

 After watching the segment, **Confucius** vents to his followers.

 **Confucius** @MasterSays
So I specialize in nothing is what they're saying. What should I specialize in? Cleaning windows, maybe? Or changing tires? I guess tires is more my thing[3].

§ Session 09.02

---

[1] Source text makes reference to Zǐhǎn 子罕 (567-544 B.C.), an interior minister of Sòng known for his kindness and impartiality. References to Zǐhǎn appear in the *Zuǒ Commentary on the Spring and Autumn Annals*, the *Familial Sayings of Confucius*, and the *Hán Fēizǐ*. Note that the interpretation given here differs from that of most traditional commentaries, which treat the character *hǎn* 罕 not as part of a name, but as an independent adverb meaning "seldom", giving the reading "Confucius seldom speaks about profit, destiny, and humanity," which contradicts known facts, as "humanity" is at the core of Confucius's moral philosophy.

[2] Source text gives commentators from the village clique of Dáxiàng, of which little more is known.

[3] Source text: "Should I drive a horse cart? Or hunt with bow and arrow? I guess the horse cart is more my thing."

Confucius @MasterSays
Baccalaureate robes used to be fashioned out of silk; these days they're mass produced in polyester[4], making them more affordable — which is a good thing. Back in the day, undergraduates would address their professors as "sir", whereas today they call you by your name[5]. I, for one, would rather my students still called me "sir".

§ Session 09.03

 Such is **Confucius** that he never assumes, never presumes, never wallows in prejudice, and never succumbs to megalomaniacal tendencies.

§ Session 09.04

---

[4] Source text: "Ceremonial caps used to be fashioned out of linen; these days people use silk (to save on cost)."

[5] Source text: "Subjects used to bow before stepping up to the throne; these days they bow only after they have ascended the steps."

 Mistaken for a crooked cop[6], **Confucius** is surrounded by an angry mob in Harlem.

 **Confucius** @MasterSays
After the fall of Rome[7], civilization as we know it rests in my hands. If God intends for the world to self-destruct, then so be it; but if civilization is meant to survive, then what could these idiots possibly do to me?

§ Session 09.05

---

[6] Mistaken for the criminal Yáng Hǔ, to whom Confucius bore an uncanny resemblance, the master is harassed (and possibly arrested or imprisoned) in the town of Kuāng, located in the state of Wèi.

[7] Source text makes reference to the golden age under the rule of King Wén of Zhōu.

Chief of Staff @WhiteHouse[8]
That master of yours — he's really something! Who would have thought he'd be so knowledgeable about so many little things.

Sly @Woodstock
Well, if he was meant to become a leader of men, the Almighty would have had good reason to equip him with a sizeable repertoire of skills, don't you think?

Confucius @MasterSays
No, no, you got it all wrong. I grew up poor and had to work many odd jobs, which explains my various abilities. If I had grown up under more favorable circumstances, I don't think I would be where I am now.

§ Session 09.06

---

[8] Source text gives the chief minister of an unnamed state.

Cameron @Locke
The master once told me that he wasn't born with a silver spoon in his mouth, so he's had to learn different skills to survive.

§ Session 09.07

Confucius @MasterSays
You think I'm some sort of genius? Far from it. When some poor soul comes to me for advice, I simply go through his options with him and help him decide on the best course of action. It's that simple.

§ Session 09.08

Confucius @MasterSays
Gone is the Star of Bethlehem. I see no Magi from the East[9]. Will there ever be a messiah?

§ Session 09.09

---

[9] Source text: "The phoenix no longer graces these shores; the Yellow River brings forth no magical chart. All is doomed." The phoenix (which heralded the reign of the mythical emperor Shùn) and the cabalistic diagrams that surfaced from the depths of the Yellow River (which, together with the trigrams of the I-Ching, ushered in the reign of the legendary sovereign Fú Xī), are both believed to be signs of the coming of a sagely ruler:

 **Confucius** yields to the blind, the deaf, the physically disabled, and those marching in a funeral procession.

§ Session 09.10

In praise of **Confucius**.

Owen @Yentl
Of your soaring intellect I stand in awe. Oh the depth of the riches of your wisdom and knowledge! How unfathomable are your deliberations and how mysterious your ways! You lead me into the inner sanctum; you teach me the workings of the universe; you show me the ways of civilized society — I cannot get enough of it! Try as I may, I cannot begin to scale the heights of your intellect, which towers above me like Mount Ararat, leaving me staring in awe[10].

§ Session 09.11

---

[10] Source text: "Having exhausted all my strength, a majestic presence towers yet before me — however hard I try, I cannot scale these heights."

 When the master's illness takes a turn for the worse, **Louie** takes it upon himself to make arrangements for an all-out state funeral, asking fellow disciples to don full military dress to impersonate honor guards. But **Confucius** soon recovers.

Confucius @MasterSays
Why go to such lengths? Why pretend to be something that you're not? Besides, it's been a while since I worked in government. I'd rather you fools carry me to my grave than have a band of cosplay soldiers drape a flag over my casket. And even if I don't get the VIP treatment, at least I have loved ones to see me off, which is more than one can ask for these days.

§ Session 09.12

Sly @Woodstock
If you come into possession of the Hope Diamond[11], do you lock it up in a vault, or sell it to the highest bidder?

Confucius @MasterSays
Sell it to the highest bidder, of course. Sell it to the highest bidder! Too bad I've yet to find someone willing to bid for my services.

§ Session 09.13

---

[11] Source text uses the image of an exquisite specimen of jade.

 **Confucius** wishes to retire to the island paradise of Palau[12].

Interlocuter @Anonymous
But can you stand to live so far removed from civilization?

Confucius @MasterSays
What do you mean, so far removed from civilization? Where I go, civilization goes with me.

§ Session 09.14

Confucius @MasterSays
Since my year abroad in Europe, I've added significantly to my collection of classical LPs, with rarities such as Wilhelm Furtwängler's Beethoven symphony cycle and Maurizio Pollini's early recordings of Chopin[13].

§ Session 09.15

---

[12] Source text has Confucius wishing to "live among the nine barbarian tribes of the East".

[13] Source text: "It was only after my return to Lǔ from the kingdom of Wèi that my understanding of music was put in perspective, as I am now able to appreciate the ceremonial functions of the Odes and the Hymns."

Confucius @MasterSays
Live up to the aspirations of your old man, and never let your coworkers down. Pay due respect to the nation's fallen heroes, and don't operate a vehicle while under the influence. How hard to do is that?

§ Session 09.16

Staring at a raging river.

Confucius @MasterSays
What is gone is gone, never to come back.

§ Session 09.17

Confucius @MasterSays
I've yet to meet someone who is turned on by good personality as much as he is turned on by good looks.

§ Session 09.18

Confucius @MasterSays
Picture a billion-dollar oil pipeline ten years in the making, awaiting government approval for the final mile. If the environmental assessment says no, I'll suspend all construction whatever the fallout. Or a trans-Atlantic hyperloop twenty years in the future, for which a working prototype has yet to be built. If it's the right investment to make, I'll give it the go-ahead regardless of cost[14].

§ Session 09.19

Confucius @MasterSays
If there's one who always does what I tell him to do, it would be Owen.

§ Session 09.20

Upon the death of **Owen**.

Confucius @MasterSays
What a shame. I mean, here was a guy who was constantly working to better himself, never taking no for an answer.

§ Session 09.21

---

[14] Source text employs the imagery of piling a mountain and flattening a plain.

Confucius @MasterSays
There are seedlings that do not stand a chance to blossom; then there are those that blossom but do not bear fruit.

§ Session 09.22

Confucius @MasterSays
Those bright young things, so full of promise! But do they measure up to the best of our generation? Wait until they reach middle age, and if they've yet to make a name for themselves, then you can write them off as pure hype.

§ Session 09.23

Confucius @MasterSays
When you're served with a stern warning, can you help but fall in line? Best to work to change your ways. When you're given a gentle reminder, aren't you overwhelmed with relief? Best to take the lesson to heart. Those who grudgingly comply with no intention of changing and those who seek relief without addressing the problem are burying their heads in the sand — God knows what to do with people like that!

§ Session 09.24

Confucius @MasterSays
Be a man of your word, make friends in higher circles, and be willing to learn from your mistakes.

§ Session 09.25

Confucius @MasterSays
Easier it is to capture the commander of an army than to win over the hearts of the common people.

§ Session 09.26

Confucius @MasterSays
Loitering on a street corner wrapped in a blanket, feeling in no way inferior to the executives waiting for the light — that's my man Louie! Like they say,

I don't care too much for money,
Money can't buy me love[15].

 **Louie** is pleased and sings the line to every passing stranger.

Confucius @MasterSays
Now, come on! It's not like you're Mother Teresa or something. It's the least you would expect of any decent human being.

§ Session 09.27

Confucius @MasterSays
It takes a harsh winter to see that pines and firs are the last of the forest giants to perish.

§ Session 09.28

Confucius @MasterSays
Good men live with a clear conscience; wise men suffer no delusions; brave men know no fear.

§ Session 09.29

---

[15] Source text quotes from the lyric "Cock Pheasant" from the *Book of Songs*, Airs of Bèi, No. 8: "I hold no grudge and harbor no greed / What harm could possibly come to me?"

Confucius @MasterSays
The guys you went to school with aren't always the ones you want to hang out with; the ones you want to hang out with aren't always the ones you want to work with; the ones you want to work with aren't always the ones you can have a heart to heart with.

§ Session 09.30

[MUSIC]
Oh kiss me and smile for me,
Tell me that you'll wait for me,
Hold me like you'll never let me go ...

I'm leaving on a jet plane,
Don't know when I'll be back again,
Oh babe I hate to go[16].

Confucius @MasterSays
If he really hates to go, he wouldn't be stepping on that jet plane in the first place.

§ Session 09.31

---

[16] Source text quotes from the popular lyrics (source unknown) "Flowers of the cherry tree / With dainty petals aflutter / How can I not think of you? / But you live so far away".

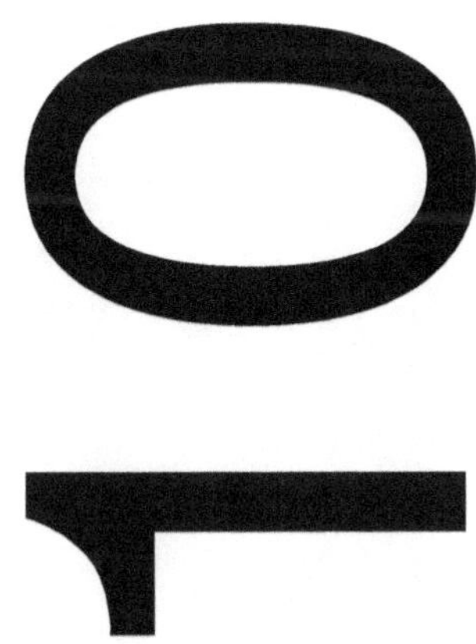

FOLKWAYS

鄉黨

When **Confucius** is with his friends he is shy and withdrawn, like he doesn't know what to say; but in church or on the debating floor words come to him, and he chooses them carefully.

§ Session 10.01

At work, he is chummy with his co-workers and respectful of his superiors. In the presence of his supervisor, he is deferential without being subservient.

§ Session 10.02

When asked to entertain foreign dignitaries, he is cordial in demeanor and professional in conduct, attending to the needs of his guests and greeting all members of the delegation with a warm smile and a firm handshake. He dresses impeccably and walks like a model on the runway[1]. When the visitors have left, he reports to the head of state and gives an account of the day's proceedings.

§ Session 10.03

---

[1] Source text gives "glides like a being with wings".

 When reporting for your first day of work at the White House, arrive early and allow yourself to be humbled by the grand premises. But don't obstruct the passageway and don't loiter in the corridors. As you approach the Oval Office, walk briskly with a sense of purpose. Fight the urge to make the odd inane comment. When you finally meet the president, show deference and listen attentively to what he has to say. Once the meeting is over, you can relax and be your old self again: the sense of relief that rushes over you as you walk out onto the West Wing is beyond words. But quickly snap out of it, for once you're back at work, it's official protocol all over again.

§ Session 10.04

When you are bearer of the Olympic torch, wield it like a royal scepter. Raise it high like the Colossus of Rhodes, or hold it close like Prometheus bearing fire[2]. When you light the Olympic flame, step up to the cauldron and carry yourself with dignity. Show to the world what an honor it is and allow yourself to relish in the moment.

§ Session 10.05

---

[2] Source text speaks of wielding a disc-shaped tablet of jade entrusted to royal envoys on diplomatic missions.

▸▸ Avoid kinky undergarments in red or purple and those with trims in contrasting tones. In the heat of summer, wear a linen slip, but always put something over it when heading out, preferably deerskin over a white slip, fox fur over a brown slip, or lambskin over a black slip. Pajama tops should come with long sleeves, which you roll up when performing chores. Nightgowns should be knee-length, over which you wear a coat of fur when receiving visitors. Accessories are *de rigueur* except when attending funerals, where you'd be wise to avoid dark caps and black trench coats. At a New Year's bash, always show up in formalwear, which should be bespoke rather than baggy — after all, we're talking about dress, not drapery.

§ Session 10.06

▶▶ At a spiritual retreat, understated elegance is the hallmark of good taste. Watch what you eat and alter your daily routine.

§ Session 10.07

▶▶ When following a diet, demand that your grains be refined and your meat diced into bite-size portions. Do not consume meat or fish that has gone bad: look out for odd coloring and foul smells. Avoid ingredients that are not in season and refuse any food that is overcooked. If the dish is made using the wrong cut of meat or doused in the wrong sauce, send it back. Never allow the flavor of meat to overpower any given entrée. When it comes to alcohol however, drink away with merry abandon, so long as you can manage to stay sober. No processed meats however, and no two buck chucks. Always clear your plate, but try not to stuff yourself.

§ Session 10.08

▶▶ Meat should never be left out overnight, and when refrigerated, consume within three days.

§ Session 10.09

▶▶ Don't talk with your mouth full, which is as distasteful as mumbling in your sleep.

§ Session 10.10

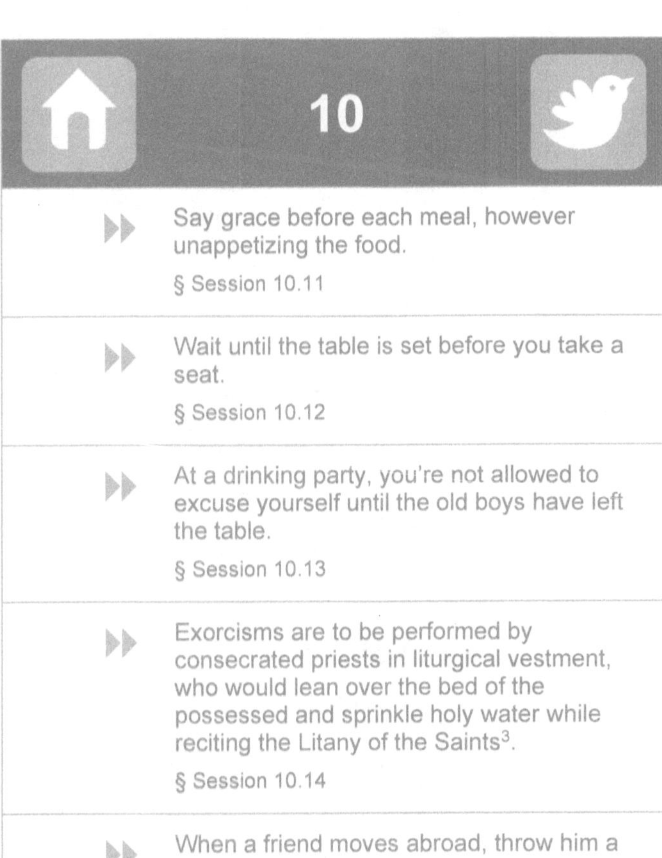

▶▶ Say grace before each meal, however unappetizing the food.

§ Session 10.11

▶▶ Wait until the table is set before you take a seat.

§ Session 10.12

▶▶ At a drinking party, you're not allowed to excuse yourself until the old boys have left the table.

§ Session 10.13

▶▶ Exorcisms are to be performed by consecrated priests in liturgical vestment, who would lean over the bed of the possessed and sprinkle holy water while reciting the Litany of the Saints[3].

§ Session 10.14

▶▶ When a friend moves abroad, throw him a farewell party and give him a ride to the airport[4].

§ Session 10.15

---

[3] Source text: "During a ritual exorcism, he would dress in full court attire and take his place on the eastern steps to observe the proceedings."

[4] Source text gives "bow twice and see him off".

>> **Cosimo de Medici** sends a packet of vitamins to **Confucius**, who signs for the package[5].

Confucius @MasterSays
No way is this stuff going down my throat. Are you crazy? It could be contaminated for all I know.

§ Session 10.16

>> Rushing to the scene of a two-alarm fire, **Confucius** asks if anyone was hurt, making no mention of pets or service animals[6].

§ Session 10.17

>> When Daddy buys you a pig-in-a-blanket, dip it in sauce and savor the bite. When Daddy buys you a holiday goose, dress it and serve it to the ones you love. When Daddy buys you a birthday pony, groom it and parade it for the world to see. At a family gathering, always say your prayers before you eat[7].

§ Session 10.18

---

[5] In the source text, Confucius receives a gift of medicinal herbs from Kāngzǐ of the Jì clan, and bows upon accepting the gift.

[6] Source text describes a fire at a stable, after which Confucius inquires after the loss of human lives but does not show any concern for the horses.

[7] Source text: "When food is bestowed upon you by the sovereign, sit tight and savor the flavor. When meat is bestowed upon you by the sovereign, grill it and offer it to those on high. When livestock is bestowed upon you by the sovereign, raise it and provide for its every need. When accompanying the sovereign at the high table, wait until offerings have been presented before commencing to eat."

▶▶ When the **Pope** visits **Confucius** at his hospital bed, the master covers up his bare flesh and has his rosary and crucifix at the ready[8].

§ Session 10.19

▶▶ When it's a matter of national security, **Confucius** takes Uber and doesn't wait for the government shuttle[9].

§ Session 10.20

▶▶ When Confucius goes to church[10], he is Mr. Inquisitive, inquiring after every detail of ritual and decorum.

§ Session 10.21

▶▶ Friendship means putting up the cost of a funeral when a friend dies broke and has no family.

§ Session 10.22

---

[8] Source text describes a visit from the sovereign as Confucius lies sick in bed, in preparation for which he dons his court robe, applies his ceremonial sash, and lies facing east as prescribed by court ritual.

[9] Source text: "When summoned by the sovereign, Confucius would just get up and go without waiting for official transport to be dispatched."

[10] Source text: "Upon entering the royal temple, he would ask about every little thing."

▶▶ Friendship means not having to say "thank you" for a gift, be it a rag doll or a race car[11], except when it is tax-deductible.

§ Session 10.23

▶▶ You don't apply makeup before going to bed; you don't act like a stranger in the privacy of your home.

§ Session 10.24

▶▶
- Always yield to the blind and hard of hearing, even if they gesture for you to go;
- Always pull over for a funeral procession, even if there's a pause in the motorcade;
- Always offer your condolences to the bereaved, even if they'd sooner be left alone;
- Always give thanks when asked to a party, even if told to make yourself at home;
- Always use caution when the weather wreak havoc, even if conditions allow for travel.

§ Session 10.25

---

[11] Source text: "When accepting a gift from a friend — be it something as valuable as a horse-drawn carriage — there is no need to bow, except in the case of sacrificial meat." Sacrificial meat, used in temple rites, is considered sacred and therefore deserving of official acknowledgement; other items are merely treated as part of the day-to-day exchange between friends.

Confucius @MasterSays
Once you're in the car, sit tight and hold on to the steering wheel[12]. Don't eye the other passengers, don't chat away, and don't point at this or that.

§ Session 10.26

Why do birds suddenly appear
Every time you are near?[13]

Louie lays down a bird snare, but the migrating fowl, as if wise to his tricks, circle around three times then fly away.

Confucius @MasterSays
Why, look at these birds! They refuse to be tempted by fate.

§ Session 10.27

---

[12] Source text: "To mount a carriage, stand straight and hold on to the guide rope."

[13] Quote of unknown provenance: "[The bird] takes to the air at the mere hint of trouble / And glides through the sky to join his flock."

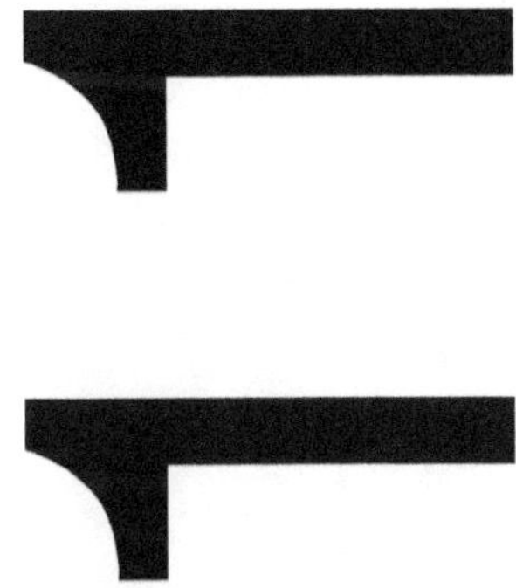

CAMARADERIE

Confucius @MasterSays
Back in the day, my followers were underprivileged youths who couldn't tell a violin from a banjo; these days I get rich kids already versed in the niceties of society. Given the choice, I'd pick the old boys over the new recruits any day.

§ Session 11.01

Confucius @MasterSays
Those who suffered with me through the Bay of Pigs invasion and the Cuban missile crisis are no longer by my side[1]. How I miss those comrades.

§ Session 11.02

Owen, Roland, Rhett, and Mason exude strength of character while Butch and Sly have mastered the art of persuasion; Auguste and Yanni dazzle us with their literary prowess while Randall and Louie are born to be leaders among men.

§ Session 11.03

---

[1] Source text: "Those who suffered with me through the ordeals of Chén and Cài are no longer by my side." The ordeals of Chén are described in Session 15.02, an episode in which Confucius and his early disciples come close to starving to death.

Confucius @MasterSays
Owen didn't exactly give me much in the way of feedback. Everything I taught him he understood and didn't require much elaboration.

§ Session 11.04

Confucius @MasterSays
Mason is a good son, no doubt about it. His parents say so, his brothers say so, and few would dispute their claims.

§ Session 11.05

Known to recite the Lord's Prayer three times a day[2], **Dixie Chet** is given the hand of the beloved niece of **Confucius**.

§ Session 11.06

---

[2] Source text describes Nán Róng (a.k.a. **Dixie Chet** @Antebellum, also see Session 05.02) as one who is known to recite "A Blemish on a Wand of Jade" three times a day, a reference to the *Book of Songs*, Major Odes, Decade of Tang, No. 2, "Frustration", which includes the lines "A blemish on a wand of jade / Can be slowly waxed away; / Harder though to erase the hurt / Of the callous things you say."

Cosimo de Medici @ilGrande
Who among your followers would you say is the most motivated to learn?

Confucius @MasterSays
Owen was as motivated a student as you'll ever find, but he is no longer of this world. As for the ones who are still around, I wouldn't quite use the word "motivated" to describe their work ethic.

§ Session 11.07

 **Confucius** is approached by the father of **Owen**, who asks the master to scrap his Cadillac to build a metal casket worthy of his son[3].

Confucius @MasterSays
Look, you feel for your son. I get it. I fell to pieces when my boy **Gil** was gunned down, even though he was nowhere near as talented as your kid. But, talent or no talent, my son didn't get the luxury treatment, and neither should yours. What's more, as a prominent government official, I need a ride to my workplace — you don't expect me to walk all the way to White House, do you?

§ Session 11.08

---

[3] In the source text, the father of the deceased asks Confucius to donate his personal chariot for use as a burial vault for his son.

Mourning the death of **Owen**.

Confucius @MasterSays
My, what a loss to this world! What a colossal loss!

§ Session 11.09

 Upon the death of **Owen**, **Confucius** is beside himself in tears. People start to point and whisper. "Look, the master's losing it!"

Confucius @MasterSays
You got that right. If this isn't a time for tremendous grief, I don't know what is.

§ Session 11.10

 Associates of **Owen** want to throw him a lavish funeral.

Confucius @MasterSays
Over my dead body you will!

They jazz up his memorial service anyway.

Confucius @MasterSays
Poor Owen! You were a son to me and I loved you like a father. You were never one for fuss or fanfare. I know you never wanted this, but I was powerless to stop it. Blame these idiots here — they were the ones insisting on doing this to you!

§ Session 11.11

Louie asks how to appease evil spirits.

Confucius @MasterSays
Why shun the company of men and seek to appease dark spirits?

Louie then asks about death.

Confucius @MasterSays
Why obsess with death when you have barely experienced life?

§ Session 11.12

 Confucius is served by **Mason**, who is respectful beyond reproach, and **Louie**, who is headstrong and fearless. Then there are **Randall** and **Sly**, who are friendly and outgoing.

Confucius @MasterSays
The likes of Louie are unlikely to live out their natural years.

§ Session 11.13

 The California State Government spends $6.4 billion on the construction of a new eastern span for the San Francisco-Oakland Bay Bridge, the most expensive public works project of its kind[4].

Ken Bukowski @Emeryville
What a waste of money! Why not just retrofit the old eastern span?

Confucius @MasterSays
The man does have a point. He doesn't say much, but when he does, he is right on the money.

§ Session 11.14

---

[4] Source text speaks of Lǔ officials wanting to tear down the old Treasury Building and erect a new one, to which Mǐn Sǔn (a.k.a. **Mason** @Withers) asks why not just renovate the old quarters rather than build anew at substantial cost.

 **Louie** plays "Heart and Soul" in a practice room at the Curtis School[5].

 **Confucius** @MasterSays
What in the name of Jesus do you think you're doing? Are you aware that you're in one of the world's top conservatories of classical music?

 Following the outburst, students in the hallway begin to cast incredulous glances at **Louie**.

 **Confucius** @MasterSays
I didn't quite mean it that way. What I meant to say was, you're no concert pianist, Louie, but you're making steady progress. Keep it up.

§ Session 11.15

---

[5] Source text begins with Confucius berating Zǐlù's (a.k.a. **Louie** @Walker) music: "How dare you bring the likes of your zither-playing into my private quarters?"

Sly @Woodstock
Between Ezra and Auguste, who is the more talented?

Confucius @MasterSays
Ezra goes overboard; Auguste doesn't quite go far enough.

Sly @Woodstock
So you're saying Ezra is more capable?

Confucius @MasterSays
I'm saying excess is just as bad, if not worse, than deficiency.

§ Session 11.16

 **Rupert Murdoch** is now worth more than the combined assets of the British royal family[6]. **Randall** has defected to his camp and serves as his financial advisor.

Confucius @MasterSays
Randall is no follower of mine. If you want to publicly denounce him, I'm not going to stop you.

§ Session 11.17

---

[6] Source text comments on how the head of the Ji clan has amassed more wealth than the emperor himself.

 **Garth** is dumb and **Jonathan** is slow, whereas **Louie** is reckless and **Ezra** is out of his mind.

§ Session 11.18

Confucius @MasterSays
Owen is quite the scholar but languishes in poverty, whereas Sly dropped out of school to launch his own startup and is making millions.

§ Session 11.19

Ezra @Johnson
People tell me I'm a nice guy. What the hell's that supposed to mean?

Confucius @MasterSays
It means you don't get on people's nerves, but you're no charmer either.

§ Session 11.20

Confucius @MasterSays
When you are moved by a person's words, you have to ask yourself: Is this guy for real, or is he just a good actor?

§ Session 11.21

Louie @Walker
If I feel like it, should I just go ahead and do it?

Confucius @MasterSays
There are other people ahead of you. Wait your turn.

Randall @RandSays
Should I just go ahead and do it?

Confucius @MasterSays
Yeah, just go ahead and do it.

Florian @Westwood
Now I'm confused here. When Louie asked, you told him to wait his turn, but when Randall asked the same question, you said to just go ahead and do it. How is that now?

Confucius @MasterSays
Randall is a scaredy cat, so I want him to step up. Louie is a show-off, so I want him to hold back.

§ Session 11.22

 Mistaken for a crooked cop, **Confucius** is surrounded by an angry mob in Harlem[7]. **Owen** is separated from the cohort in the ensuing chaos, then later rejoins the group.

Confucius @MasterSays:
Thank God — for a minute I thought you were dead!

Owen @Yentl
That's not possible. I still have a job to do. I have to look after you, don't I?

§ Session 11.23

---

[7] The passage refers to an incident where Confucius, mistaken for a common criminal, is harassed and imprisoned in the town of Kuāng, the details of which are given in Session 09.05.

Lorenzo de Medici @ilMagnifico
Would you consider Louie and Randall exemplary statesmen?

Confucius @MasterSays
For a minute I thought you had something important to ask me — I wasn't expecting you to yak about these two chumps. You see, to me, a statesman is someone who does what's right and is willing to walk away when things smell fishy. By this measure, Louie and Randall still have a ways to go. I'd say they're career politicians, but not quite up there with the Jeffersons and Churchills.

Lorenzo de Medici @ilMagnifico
So you're saying they're essentially goons at the beck and call of their political masters?

Confucius @MasterSays
I wouldn't quite put it that way. I mean, if you tell them to slaughter their own kinsfolk or assassinate the president, I'm sure they'd refuse.

§ Session 11.24

 **Louie** appoints twelve-year-old **Garth** as deputy sheriff of Fairfax[8].

Confucius @MasterSays
But the kid is still in school!

Louie @Walker
He'll learn all he needs to know on the job. He'll learn how to apprehend criminals and book them into lockup, and will also be trained to handle citizen complaints and write police reports. Who says learning can only take place in the classroom?

Confucius @MasterSays
How I hate those smart alecks who have an answer for everything!

§ Session 11.25

 In the company of **Louie**, **Randall**, **Florian**, and **Jonah**.

Confucius @MasterSays
I'm from an older generation, and I know you all have misgivings about people my age. What do they know, you must be thinking. But suppose they knew better, and wanted to make use of your talents — what would you be able to offer?

---

[8] Source text: Zǐlù (a.k.a. **Louie** @Walker) appoints Zǐgāo (a.k.a. **Garth** @Lamb), who is young and inexperienced, as steward of the Bì estate.

Louie @Walker
Give me a starving third world country caught in the crossfires of two warring superpowers. Put me in charge and I'll make a brave and upstanding citizen out of every man and woman[9].

Confucius @MasterSays sneers.
What about you, Randall?

Randall @RandSays
Give me a tiny city state, and I'll see to it that everyone is fed, if not clothed and schooled.

Confucius @MasterSays
And you, Florian?

Florian @Westwood
Me — can't say I can do much, as I'm still learning the ropes. But parachute me into an important occasion, like a party convention or a presidential debate, and I'd love to play host so I can dress up and look dashing on camera[10].

---

[9] Source text: "Give me a nation of a mere thousand chariots, sandwiched between two mighty powers, besieged by war and plagued by famine. In no more than three years, I'll turn every man and woman into an upstanding citizen who isn't afraid to fight for his country.

[10] Source text: "At a meeting between heads of state, let me put on my cap and gown, and be the one to officiate."

Confucius @MasterSays
And you, Jonah?

 Jonah gives his guitar[11] a long strum, then sits straight and replies in all earnestness.

Jonah @White
I see things a little differently from these three dudes.

Confucius @MasterSays
That's perfectly alright. We're just sharing personal fantasies here.

Jonah @White
I'm just thinking, in late spring, when the weather's warmer, let's get a couple of guys together, and maybe round up a few kids, and we can all go down to the beach for a swim, then dry off on the pier, and get totally drunk and sing rugby songs all the way home[12].

Confucius heaves a long sigh.

Confucius @MasterSays
I'm with Jonah on this.

---

[11] In the source text Zēng Diǎn (a.k.a. **Jonah** @White) strums his zither.

[12] Source text: "In late spring, when spring outfits become available, let's round up five to six young men and six to seven children and head for the River Yí, where we'll bathe and then dry off on the rain dance platform, and sing all the way home."

Jonah @White
So what do you make of their comments?

Confucius @MasterSays
They're just thinking out loud, that's all.

Jonah @White
Then why'd you sneer at Louie?

Confucius @MasterSays
I sneered because he's so brash. You need a certain aplomb to go into politics, don't you think?

Jonah @White
And Randall — he wanted to go into politics too, didn't he?

Confucius @MasterSays
He did say "Give me a tiny city state", did he not?

Jonah @White
And Florian too?

Confucius @MasterSays
How else would you be able to host a party convention? But if he's content merely to moderate the debate, who's going to run the country?

§ Session 11.26

HUMANITY

顔淵

Owen asks how to become a better person.

 **Confucius** @MasterSays
Keep your personal perversions in check and return to common decency. If for one day you could banish those unholy thoughts, the world would be a better place. And no one can do it for you — this is a demon you'll have to face down on your own.

Owen @Yentl
How do I rid myself of these perversions?

Confucius @MasterSays
See no evil, hear no evil, speak no evil, and do no evil.

Owen @Yentl
That's a lot to take in, but I'll give it my best shot.

§ Session 12.01

Roland asks how to become a better person.

Confucius @MasterSays
Live each day like it's your royal coronation, and treat each passer-by like she's the Queen of the England[1]. Don't do to others what you don't want them to do to you. Keep to this golden rule, and you'll be worshipped like royalty at home and abroad.

Roland @Archer
Whoa, that's a tall order, but I'll give it a go.

§ Session 12.02

---

[1] Source text: "Step out into the world like you're greeting a royal dignitary and address your people like you're hosting a magnificent ceremony."

 **Seymour** asks about becoming a better person.

Confucius @MasterSays
A better person is one who holds back on his speech.

Seymour @McKnight
You've got to be kidding! Holding back on your speech makes you a better person?

Confucius @MasterSays
Look at it this way. You have a hard enough time completing even the simplest of tasks. Don't you think you should hold back a little on the big talk?

§ Session 12.03

 **Seymour** asks about becoming a well-rounded individual.

 **Confucius** @MasterSays
A well-rounded individual is one who fears nothing and has few worries on his mind.

Seymour @McKnight
So if you don't lose sleep and nothing spooks you, you're considered a well-rounded person?

Confucius @MasterSays
Look at it this way. When you live with a clear conscience, what is there to fear? What is there to keep you up at night?

§ Session 12.04

Seymour is in a state of manic depression.

Seymour @McKnight
Say, you all have brothers to lean on, but I don't!

Auguste @LeMerchant
Listen to me, Seymour. The Lord alone knows what plans he has for you. Like they say, "Life and death are the work of fate; riches and glory are in the hands of God". You cannot change the circumstances of your birth, but from then on you're fully in charge. Learn to hold a steady job and treat your fellow humans with respect. And when you do, who's not going to want to be your bro, eh?

§ Session 12.05

Ezra asks what it means to have clarity of mind.

Confucius @MasterSays
When insinuations don't cloud your judgment and malicious slander doesn't shake your faith, you can be said to have clarity of mind. For when insinuations fail to unnerve you and slander doesn't change your position on issues, you are looking beyond the immediate distractions and focusing on the bigger picture.

§ Session 12.06

Confucius @MasterSays
Feed them, arm them, and earn their trust.

Sly @Woodstock
And if we had to drop one of the three, which would it be?

Confucius @MasterSays
Arms.

Sly @Woodstock
And if we had to drop yet another?

Confucius @MasterSays
Food. Think about it: we're all going to die at some point, but that bond of trust is what holds the community together.

§ Session 12.07

Guy Duchamps @Ministre
What use is decorum in an age where the public favors candor and openness? Decorum is vastly overrated.

Sly @Woodstock
Now that is a misstatement. I'd take it back if I were you. Presentation is just as important as substance. If appearances don't matter, then why dress in that cashmere sweater? Wouldn't acrylic be just as functional, if not more so? And those sheepskin boots you're wearing — do you really think they're better value than nylon?

§ Session 12.08

King Maximilian @LastKnight
Come famine and fiscal shortage, what do you do?

Hubert @EubieSays
Issue a tax break.

King Maximilian @LastKnight
But I barely have enough — how do I make do with less?

Hubert @EubieSays
When your people are affluent, how can the government not be well-stocked? When your constituents are struggling, how can you bear to live the good life?

§ Session 12.09

Ezra @Johnson
I'd like to become a conscientious and balanced individual.

Confucius @MasterSays
You're conscientious when you're committed to a cause and can bring yourself to do right by other people. Balance, on the other hand, is about not letting your rage get the better of you to the point where you're sweet one minute and screaming the next[2], you know, like the Katy Perry song[3]:

You're hot then you're cold,
You're yes then you're no,
You're in then you're out,
You're up then you're down,

Now that would be really losing it.

§ Session 12.10

---

[2] Source text: "You want him alive one minute and dead the next. Now he can't be both alive and dead, can he?"

[3] Source text quotes the *Book of Songs*, Minor Odes, Fourth Decade, No. 4, "I Walk These Lonely Fields": "You leave me not for riches and wealth / but because you fell for someone else."

Louis XIV seeks advice on leadership.

Confucius @MasterSays
Expect leaders to lead and followers to follow; allow parents to parent and kids to kid around.

Louis XIV @theSunKing
Good point. If leaders don't lead and followers don't follow, if parents don't parent and kids don't kid around, what kind of crazy world do we live in, anyway?

§ Session 12.11

 Louie, while serving as district court judge, rarely deliberates overnight before handing down a sentence.

Confucius @MasterSays
I know of few arbiters of the law so eager to hand down a sentence based on only partial testimony. Would it hurt to wait a day or two before reaching a conclusion?

§ Session 12.12

Confucius @MasterSays
In a court of law, my judgment is no better than that of the next person. What I would really like to do is to get rid of litigation altogether.

§ Session 12.13

Ezra seeks advice on leadership.

Confucius @MasterSays
Dedicate yourself to a cause and pursue it with all your heart.

§ Session 12.14

Confucius @MasterSays
Read extensively and learn proper etiquette, and you more or less have your future mapped out for you.

§ Session 12.15

Confucius @MasterSays
Good people champion worthy causes and want no part in shady dealings; unsavory types profit through shady business and balk at donating to charity.

§ Session 12.16

Cosimo de Medici seeks advice on leadership.

Confucius @MasterSays
Leaders lead by example. If you go down the straight path, who among your followers would dare stray?

§ Session 12.17

 **Cosimo de Medici** sees **Confucius** for advice on home security.

Confucius @MasterSays
If it weren't for your greed, what could a burglar possibly want from you?

§ Session 12.18

Cosimo de Medici @ilGrande
What do you say we kill all the bad guys so that only the good guys are left?

Confucius @MasterSays
Why the need to kill? When you're a good guy, they'll all want to play for the good team. You see, the actions of the ruler set an example that ripples across the land; the people at the grassroots have no choice but to bow to the trend.

§ Session 12.19

Ezra @Johnson
What does it take to succeed in life?

Confucius @MasterSays
Depends on what you mean by "succeed".

Ezra @Johnson
You succeed when you become a household name in this country and abroad.

Confucius @MasterSays
What you're describing is celebrity, not success. Success is when you listen with an attentive ear and cater to the needs of those you serve, in the process promoting fairness and social justice; whereas celebrity has to do with appearing to be godly and gracious and convincing yourself that you are, dismissing all evidence to the contrary — now that's how you become a household name in this country and abroad.

§ Session 12.20

Francis accompanies Confucius to the pier.

Francis @Waite
How do I grow the good and root out the evil in me? How do I remain clear-headed through it all?

Confucius @MasterSays
You put duty before pleasure — that's how you grow the good. You blame yourself and not other people for the disappointments in your life — that's how you root out the evil. As for clarity of mind, never for a minute allow your anger to simmer to the point where you put your personal safety and the lives of others at risk — now that would be really messed up.

§ Session 12.21

Francis asks how to be good.

Confucius @MasterSays
Love your fellow man.

Francis asks how to be wise.

Confucius @MasterSays
Know your fellow man.

Francis is perplexed.

Confucius @MasterSays
Allow those with merit to rise to the top, and the doubters and dissenters will fall in line.

Francis later runs into **Auguste**.

Francis @Waite
Earlier the master was telling me that if I allow those with merit to rise to the top, the doubters and dissenters would fall in line. What is that supposed to mean?

Auguste @LeMerchant
What an insightful comment! When Steve Jobs retired from Apple, he handed the company over to Tim Cook, who turned it into the most profitable business in the world. After Louis Vuitton merged with Moët Hennessy, it hired Marc Jacobs as artistic director, who breathed new life into a stuffy old fashion house on its way into oblivion[4].

§ Session 12.22

---

[4] Source text: "When the mythical emperor Shùn was in power, he singled out Gāo Yáo from the masses, and all the unsavory characters made a hasty retreat. When Shāng dynasty founder Tāng was in power, he singled out Yī Yǐn from the masses, and all the undesirables knew it was time to go."

Sly seeks advice on friendship.

Confucius @MasterSays
Give it to them straight, and tell it to them nicely. If they can't take the truth, that's their problem — you've done your part.

§ Session 12.23

Jonathan @JonoSays
Accomplished individuals move in cultured circles, where they forge friendships that advance their spiritual well-being.

§ Session 12.24

LEADERSHIP

Louie seeks advice on leadership.

Confucius @MasterSays
Show them how it's done and put them to work.

Louie @Walker
That's it?

Confucius @MasterSays
And keep at it.

§ Session 13.01

 As administrator of the Bank of Medici, **Roland** seeks advice on personnel matters[1].

Confucius @MasterSays
Establish a standard protocol, let bygones be bygones, and seek out the talent.

Roland @Archer
How am I supposed to know where the talent is?

Confucius @MasterSays
Go for the obvious — talent that you can see. As for what you cannot see, somebody's bound to discover it sooner or later.

§ Session 13.02

---

[1] **Roland** @Archer is appointed steward of the Jì clan.

Louie @Walker
So if the Governor of Virginia were to let you run things around here, where would you start?[2]

Confucius @MasterSays
I'd see to it that everything is addressed by its proper name.

Louie @Walker
How stupid is that? What good would that do?

Confucius @MasterSays
Boy are you ignorant — better to keep your mouth shut when you don't have anything intelligent to say!

---

[2] Source text: "If the (newly crowned) King of Wèi were to seek your advice in political matters, where would you start?"

Confucius @MasterSays
You see, when names are ill-fitting, language is less than precise; when instructions are imprecise, work fails to meet standards; when work is substandard, civilizations crumble. In a world less than civilized people have little regard for the law, and when lawlessness reigns, it's every man for himself. Which is why a gentleman chooses his words carefully, making sure the name matches the referent so that his language is precise, guaranteeing that his work is of the highest standard.

§ Session 13.03

 **Francis** approaches **Confucius** for tips on farming.

Confucius @MasterSays
You're better off asking a farmer.

Francis asks **Confucius** for tips on gardening.

Confucius @MasterSays
Best to consult a professional gardener.

 After **Francis** leaves, **Confucius** vents to his followers.

 **Confucius** @MasterSays
What an idiot! Show them fairness and they'll have faith in you; demand discipline and they'll defer to you; be a man of your word and they'll lay down their lives for you; and when your reputation spreads far and wide, you'll be surrounded by a passionately loyal following. People will come to you from near and far, brain surgeons and rocket scientists, not to mention farmers and gardeners. By then will you really need to roll up your sleeves and do your own farm work? Go figure.

§ Session 13.04

Confucius @MasterSays
I know a guy who can recite every line of Shakespeare by heart[3] and yet can't hold down a lowly managerial position. You send him on a consular mission and he's at a loss as to what to do. Makes you wonder, what good is knowing so much Shakespeare?

§ Session 13.05

Confucius @MasterSays
With the proper mandate, your wishes are carried out without as much as a hint; without the proper mandate, you'll be shouting your lungs out and no one will listen to you.

§ Session 13.06

Confucius @MasterSays
Britain and the United States are joined in a special relationship[4].

§ Session 13.07

---

[3] Source text: "one who can recite the three hundred verses of the *Book of Songs*".

[4] Source text refers to the states of Lǔ and Wèi, whose respective founders were brothers (princes of the Zhōu royal house) with similar leadership styles, who ultimately met similar fates.

Commenting on Facebook founder **Mark Zuckerburg**[5].

Confucius @MasterSays
The man is a connoisseur of the simple life. When he bought his first Honda, his reasoning was that it was "a good fit". When the dealership offered him complimentary upgrades, he said, "That's more than enough." When the car company decided to throw in a luxury package, his reaction was, "Man, that is more than I could ever dream of!"

§ Session 13.08

---

[5] In the source text, Confucius commends Prince Jīng of Wèi for his fiscal discipline and his fondness for the simple life.

 With **Randall** in attendance, **Confucius** travels to the Bangladeshi capital of Dhaka[6].

Confucius @MasterSays
My oh my, look at all these people!

Randall @RandSays
Yes, the place is full to the brim. What can I do for them?

Confucius @MasterSays
You can raise their standard of living.

Randall @RandSays
And after they become reasonably prosperous, then what?

Confucius @MasterSays
You educate them.

§ Session 13.09

---

[6] In the source text, Confucius travels to the state of Wèi.

Confucius @MasterSays
Hire me and see results in a year; in three, expect to see a world of difference.

§ Session 13.10

Imagine there's no countries,
It isn't hard to do.
Nothing to kill or die for,
And no religion too.

Confucius @MasterSays
70 years of European economic cooperation has effectively wiped out the prospect of war among the nations of Western Europe. How wise! How so very wise![7]

§ Session 13.11

Confucius @MasterSays
With even the brightest of leaders at the helm, it'll be a generation or more before the fortunes of a nation can be turned around.

§ Session 13.12

---

[7] Source text quotes a saying of unknown provenance: "Put a nation in the hands of a worthy leader for a good hundred years, and you can expect it to be rid of slaughter and bloodshed altogether."

Confucius @MasterSays
If you're morally sound, you'll have nothing to fear on the campaign trail; if you're morally unsound, how can you get people to come around to your view?

§ Session 13.13

Randall returns from work.

Confucius @MasterSays
Why so late today?

Randall @RandSays
I was tied up with business.

Confucius @MasterSays
Business? Or personal matters? Though I look to be retired, if there was any important business that needed attention, don't you think I would have heard about it?

§ Session 13.14

King Frederick @SleepyHead
What kind of words would inspire a nation to greatness?

Confucius @MasterSays
If only there was such a thing! But the Shakespearean line "uneasy lies the head that wears a crown" comes close[8], and should serve as a reminder of the challenges of leadership and the demands it makes of the head of state.

King Frederick @SleepyHead
And what kind of dumbass talk would run the country into the ground?

Confucius @MasterSays
Again, not quite so dramatically, but I'd be wary of monarchs who tout the line "trust and obey, there's no other way[9]". Rousseau rightly observed that "obedience is due only to legitimate powers". If the leader is wise and his subjects defer, the result may not be so bad; but if the leader is misguided and his people follow blindly, surely the nation is headed down a path to ruin.

§ Session 13.15

---

[8] Source text: "Hard it is to be king, no less difficult to be a subject of the king."

[9] Source text: "I derive no joy from being king other than the fact that people must do whatever I say."

Ole McCoy seeks advice on leadership.

Confucius @MasterSays
If you build it they will come.

§ Session 13.16

▶▶ As governor of Georgia, **Auguste** seeks advice on leadership[10].

Confucius @MasterSays
Don't force things, and don't fret over the bottom line. Forced results will only come back to haunt you; agonizing over the bottom line obscures the bigger picture.

§ Session 13.17

---

[10] Source text: **Auguste** @LeMerchant is appointed as steward of Jŭfŭ.

Ole McCoy @Appalachia
Where I come from, people are conscientious to a fault, like the son who turned his own father in for stealing a car.

Confucius @MasterSays
That's not how things are done where I come from. Fathers cover for their sons, and sons cover for their fathers. That's what I call conscientious.

§ Session 13.18

Francis asks about becoming a better person.

Confucius @MasterSays
Carry yourself with dignity, treat others with respect, and show dedication to your work. You can travel to the ends of the earth and still be held to these expectations.

§ Session 13.19

Sly @Woodstock
What does it take to rise to the ranks of the salaried classes?

Confucius @MasterSays
Carry yourself with dignity, and when dispatched to the far corners of the earth, show that you're able to advance the national interest and represent your government favorably.

Sly @Woodstock
And failing that, what is the next best thing?

Confucius @MasterSays
The next best thing is to be beloved of all members of your extended family and trusted by the locals in your community.

Sly @Woodstock
And if that isn't possible, what then?

Confucius @MasterSays
If you could be a man of your word and get the job done quickly, then I suppose, mediocre as you are, you might still be worth your salt.

Sly @Woodstock
What about those politicians currently serving office? Are they worth the public dime?

Confucius @MasterSays
Oh, those small-minded sycophants — don't even get me started.

§ Session 13.20

Confucius @MasterSays
Think of extremists and pessimists as people who miss the mark somewhat. Extremists go too far; pessimists fall shy of the target.

§ Session 13.21

Confucius @MasterSays
My doctor at the Southern Methodist Hospital used to tell me, "Without grit and perseverance, you'll never get into medical school[11]". He was right. Didn't Shakespeare once say that "perseverance keeps honor bright[12]"? But I'm sure you don't need Shakespeare to tell you that.

§ Session 13.22

Confucius @MasterSays
Guys get along without trying too hard; try as they may, wimps just cannot get along.

§ Session 13.23

---

[11] Source text: "They have a saying down south, 'If you can't keep at it, you ain't gon become no witch doctor'."

[12] Source text quotes from the *I-Ching* (a.k.a. *Book of Changes*): "Do your best to persevere, or humiliation will draw near."

Sly @Woodstock
What do you think of heroes who are universally loved?

Confucius @MasterSays
I don't think much of them.

Sly @Woodstock
What about villains who are universally feared?

Confucius @MasterSays
I don't think much of them either. I'd take more seriously names that are revered by the most well-regarded households and crooks that are feared by the most bloodcurdling thugs.

§ Session 13.24

Confucius @MasterSays
A good boss is easy to work for but hard to appease — pander to his whims and he'll see right through the ruse. But on the job, expect him to bring out the best in you. A bad boss is hard to work for but easy to appease — the smallest of petty favors will get you on his good side. But don't be surprised when he milks you for all you're worth.

§ Session 13.25

Confucius @MasterSays
Cool dudes are self-assured without looking pretentious; dorks act pretentious and yet exude no confidence.

§ Session 13.26

Confucius @MasterSays
Good men come in the guise of impassioned, headstrong, inarticulate dorks.

§ Session 13.27

Louie @Walker
How do you adjust to life as a public figure?

Confucius @MasterSays
Learn to draw the line between the personal and the professional. Put on the charm for your wider audience but be who you really are in front of those you love.

§ Session 13.28

Confucius @MasterSays
Put a capable person in charge for seven years and the country should be able to defend itself.

§ Session 13.29

Confucius @MasterSays
To urge untrained civilians onto the battlefield is to send these people to their deaths.

§ Session 13.30

4

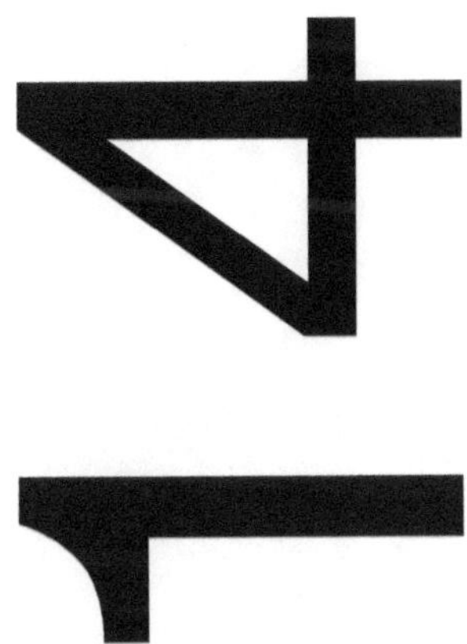

HUMILITY

憲問

 **Shane** seeks an illustration of shameful behavior.

Confucius @MasterSays
Good for you if you make a fortune when most everyone has achieved the American dream, but shame on you if you're a billionaire when the ninety-nine percent cannot make ends meet.

§ Session 14.01

Shane @McEwan
If we could do away with ambition, pride, jealousy, and greed, would it make for a better world?

Confucius @MasterSays
It would make for quite a spectacle, but I can't say it would make for a better world.

§ Session 14.02

Confucius @MasterSays
An intellectual with only creature comforts on his mind does not deserve to be called an intellectual.

§ Session 14.03

Confucius @MasterSays
In civilized society, you're free to speak your mind and do as you like; in less civilized places, people say one thing and do another.

§ Session 14.04

Confucius @MasterSays
Words come naturally to those with the moral prerogative, but not all those who have a way with words are morally superior. Courage comes naturally to those defending a just cause, but not all displays of valor represent a cause that is just.

§ Session 14.05

Dixie Chet @Antebellum
Napoleon was conqueror of the world; Hitler struck fear in the eyes of his foes — and yet they met disgraceful ends, whereas Clinton and Gore simply fixed the economy, and are now remembered as the architects of lasting peace[1].

 Confucius is silent. After **Dixie Chet** leaves, he comments:

Confucius @MasterSays
The guy's real sharp.

§ Session 14.06

---

[1] Source text: "Yì exhibited legendary marksmanship, Ào the strength to raise an ark, the likes of which the world has never seen, only to die terrible deaths. Yǔ and Jì tended to such mundane matters as farming and irrigation and are remembered as architects of lasting peace."

Confucius @MasterSays
Worthy men are known to have lapses of judgment; unworthy men seldom ever exhibit good judgment.

§ Session 14.07

Confucius @MasterSays
If you truly love a person, can you bring yourself not to nag him? If you're a true friend, can you help but say what he doesn't want to hear?

§ Session 14.08

Confucius @MasterSays
In Britain, bills are introduced by the Prime Minister's cabinet, then scrutinized by the House of Lords and the House of Commons before they are sent to the Queen for Royal Assent and become the law of the land[2].

§ Session 14.09

---

[2] Source text describes the layers of oversight that go into the production of high level communications in the state of Zhèng, known for its diplomatic prowess: "Before issuing an official communique, Bì Chén would produce an initial draft to be critiqued by Shì Shú and embellished by Zǐ Yǔ before it is turned over to Zǐ Chǎn of Dōnglǐ for a final revision."

Confucius is asked what he thinks of Alaric[3].

Confucius @MasterSays
The man is a charitable leader.

Interlocuter @Anonymous
What about Attila[4]?

Confucius @MasterSays
Now we all know what he is like.

Interlocuter @Anonymous
And Aetius[5]?

Confucius @MasterSays
Now there's a man for you! Aetius robbed Bonifacius of his rightful place and rallied Hun armies to march on Rome. Yet few historians question his contributions to the empire.

§ Session 14.10

---

[3] In the source text, Confucius is asked his opinion of Zǐ Chǎn, minister of the state of Zhèng.

[4] Confucius is asked his opinion of Prince Shēn of Chǔ (a.k.a. Zǐ Xī), an otherwise virtuous individual who was instrumental in blocking an offer of employment for Confucius in the court of his father, King Zhāo of Chǔ.

[5] Confucius is asked his opinion of Guǎn Zhòng, famed minister of the state of Qí, whom he regards fondly, citing the example of Guǎn confiscating some three hundred properties belonging to the Bó clan and forcing clan members to subsist on morsels, punishment about which the head of the clan, to the end of his life, never dared utter a word of complaint.

Confucius @MasterSays
Easier it is to be rich and not conceited than to be poor but not resentful.

§ Session 14.11

Confucius @MasterSays
Dianne Feinstein would make a good mayor of New York or San Francisco, but would have trouble winning votes in the Ozarks or rural Alabama[6].

§ Session 14.12

---

[6] Source text: "The likes of Mèng Gōngchuò (minister of Lǔ known for his stoicism) would excel as steward of a large estate like Zhào or Wèi, but would struggle as minister of a small state like Téng or Xuē.

Louie @Walker
What would it take for somebody to be considered "the complete package"?

Confucius @MasterSays
He would have to have the brains of Einstein and the brawn of Rambo, plus the humility of Gandhi and the charm of James Bond, not to mention a Hamptons upbringing and an Ivy League degree[7].

Confucius @MasterSays
Or if that is too much to ask, maybe we can just go with someone who isn't blinded by greed, who steps up when duty calls, and who can be counted on to keep his word — that, to me, is the complete package.

§ Session 14.13

---

[7] Source text: "He would have to have the deliberation of Zāng Wǔzhòng (see Session 14.15), the dispassion of Mèng Gōngchuò (see Session 14.12), the derring-do of Biàn Zhuāngzǐ (legendary warrior), and the diplomacy of Rǎn Qiú (a.k.a. **Randall** @RandSays), not to mention mastery of decorum and knowledge of the arts."

 Confucius speaks to White House Chief-of-Staff **Henry Halleck** and asks after **Abraham Lincoln**[8].

Confucius @MasterSays
Is it true that the president never speaks, never smiles, and never receives gifts?

Henry Halleck @OldBrains
That is something of an exaggeration. The president speaks only when he has something to say, smiles only when he is genuinely moved, and receives gifts only when he deems it proper. That way people appreciate what he has to say, cherish the occasional smile, and are willing to give generously.

Confucius @MasterSays
How extraordinary! How truly extraordinary!

§ Session 14.14

---

[8] Source text: "Confucius speaks to Gōngmíng Jiǎ and inquires after his late master Gōngshú Wénzǐ (former minister of the state of Wèi, rumored to be the embodiment of perfection).

Confucius @MasterSays
Early settlers used guns, cash, and whiskey to acquire land from Indian tribes. Though some say the Indians were never coerced, I have my doubts[9].

§ Session 14.15

Confucius @MasterSays
Rousseau believed in bluntness and baring all; Machiavelli excelled at cunning and duplicity[10].

§ Session 14.16

---

[9] In the source text, Confucius describes how the exiled minister Zāng Wǔzhòng (see Session 14.13) surreptitiously returns to his family stronghold of Fáng and, using his occupation of the walled city as leverage, asks the King of Lǔ to appoint a close family member as successor of his estate. Though a polite request was made of the king, Zāng's *de facto* occupation of the city meant that his overlord effectively had no choice but to give in to his wishes.

[10] Source text: "King Huán of Qí believed in bluntness and baring all; King Wén of Jìn excelled at cunning and duplicity."

Louie @Walker
When Johannes was besieged by Valentinian at Ravenna, Castinus was captured and sent into exile, whereas Aetius switched allegiance and sided with the usurper — what a heartless traitor, this Aetius![11]

Confucius @MasterSays
That's no way to look at it. Valentinian united the Eastern and Western empires without war or bloodshed, to which he has Aetius to thank. A lifesaver he is, this Aetius, a lifesaver[12].

§ Session 14.17

---

[11] Source text: "When Prince Jiū of Qí was assassinated by his half brother Xiǎobái (who later became King Huán of Qí), the prince's minister Zhāo Hū took his own life, whereas his other minister Guǎn Zhòng did not follow suit. How heartless of him!"

[12] Source text: "King Huán of Qí united the feudal kings without resorting to force, to which he has Guǎn Zhòng to thank. A man with a big heart he is, this Guǎn Zhòng, a man with a big heart."

Sly @Woodstock
You call Aetius a hero? When Johannes was slain by Valentinian, not only did Aetius not avenge his master, he ended up working for the mastermind behind the coup[13].

Confucius @MasterSays
Aetius made peace with Valentinian and rallied the Romans to defeat the Huns. And the Western world was all the better for it. If it weren't for Aetius, we would all be barbarians on horseback feasting on raw flesh. Faced with the same prospects, a lesser individual might have taken his life out of shame, but not Aetius — he sees the bigger picture[14].

§ Session 14.18

---

[13] Source text: "This Guǎn Zhòng character is really a piece of work, wouldn't you say? When his master Prince Jiū was killed at the hands of his half brother Xiǎobái (who later became King Huán of Qí), not only did Guǎn Zhòng refuse to take his own life, he ended up serving as minister to the usurper King Huán."

[14] Source text: "With Guǎn Zhòng at the helm, King Huán of Qí was able to unite the feudal kings, and the world is all the better for it. Why, if it weren't for Guǎn Zhòng, we'd still be wearing our hair long and buttoning our robes on the wrong side (as do barbaric tribes outside of the sphere of Chinese cultural dominance)."

 **Paul McCartney** was presented with a British Empire medal in 1965 alongside band members **Richard Starkey**, **George Harrison**, and **John Lennon**. In 1997, McCartney was knighted by the **Queen of England**[15].

 **Confucius** @MasterSays
He is now "Sir" Paul McCartney[16].

§ Session 14.19

---

[15] Source text: "Gōngshú Wénzǐ (also see Session 14.14), together with his steward Zhuàn, was promoted to the rank of minister."

[16] Source text: "He is truly deserving of the appellation 'Wén' (sophisticated; cultured)."

 Confucius complains about the autocratic tendencies of **Ivan the Terrible**.

Cosimo de Medici @ilGrande
So why hasn't Russia been run into the ground?

Confucius @MasterSays
With the rich tapestry of Russian traditions, the long arm of Russian diplomacy, and the formidable size of the Russian army, Russia is never going to be run into the ground[17].

§ Session 14.20

Confucius @MasterSays
If he promises the world, it's too good to be true.

§ Session 14.21

---

[17] Source text quotes Confucius describing King Líng of Wèi as barbaric, to which Kāngzǐ asks why the state of Wèi is still standing. Confucius answers that Wèi is able to avoid collapse due to the efforts of its talented ministers: the diplomatic savvy of Zhòngshú Yù (a.k.a. Kǒng Wénzǐ – see Session 05.15 on his efforts at literary mastery), the religious authority of Zhù Tuó (see Session 06.16 on his eloquence), and the military prowess of Wángsūn Jiǎ.

Russia annexes the Crimea. **Confucius** suits up and heads to the White House to request action[18].

Obama @44th_president
Go ask Congress for authorization.

Confucius @MasterSays
Okay, but I just want you to know that, as a trusted adviser, I have the obligation to tell you what I believe to be the best course of action.

Confucius then presents his case to the House and the Senate, which both say no.

Confucius @MasterSays
Well then, I've done my part. As national adviser, I have the obligation to tell you what I truly think.

§ Session 14.22

Louie asks how to serve the leader of a nation.

Confucius @MasterSays
Be blunt. Never hold back on the truth.

§ Session 14.23

---

[18] Source text describes how when minister Chén Chéngzǐ (a.k.a. Tián Héng) assassinates King Jiǎn of Qí, Confucius pleads with King Āi of Lǔ to send in troops to intervene in the politics of their neighboring state.

Confucius @MasterSays
Honorable men deal above the table;
shady characters deal under the table.

§ Session 14.24

Confucius @MasterSays
Time was when people read to amuse
themselves; nowadays it's to show off to
others.

§ Session 14.25

 **Confucius** gives audience to a messenger of
St Augustine of Hippo[19].

Confucius @MasterSays
So, how is the Bishop keeping himself?

Messenger @SaintAugustine
He is committing to paper his regrets for
having led a sinful and immoral life.

After the departure of the messenger:

Confucius @MasterSays
That was quite a powerful message!

§ Session 14.26

---

[19] Source text describes a visit by a messenger of Qú Bóyù (also see
Session 15.06), a minister of Wèi known for his sound judgment.

Confucius @MasterSays
If it's none of your business, stay out of it.

§ Session 14.27

Jonathan @JonoSays
Never seek to act outside of your authority.

§ Session 14.28

Confucius @MasterSays
Don't ever promise more than you can deliver.

§ Session 14.29

Confucius @MasterSays
Good men live with a clear conscience; wise men suffer no delusions; brave men know no fear. How I wish I could be more like them.

Sly @Woodstock
For a minute I thought you were talking about yourself.

§ Session 14.30

 **Sly** is given to making frivolous comparisons of his peers.

Confucius @MasterSays
I'm sure he has his reasons, but I, for one, have better things to do with my time.

§ Session 14.31

Confucius @MasterSays
Worry not about getting your fifteen minutes of fame, but about whether you have what it takes to make it big.

§ Session 14.32

Confucius @MasterSays
Neither gullible nor overly paranoid, yet instinctively cautious when people are up to something funny — that's what I call street smarts.

§ Session 14.33

Peewee @Misanthrope
What's with this flitting from flame to flame like a hungry moth? If I didn't know better, I'd say you were prostituting yourself to anyone with power and influence!

Confucius @MasterSays
Prostitute, no, but loyalty is overrated, don't you think?

§ Session 14.34

Confucius @MasterSays
What sets the thoroughbred apart is not just its physical strength, but its superior discipline.

§ Session 14.35

Interlocuter @Anonymous
Turn the other cheek, answer hate with love, so they say. You agree?

Confucius @MasterSays
Answer hate with love? Then how would you answer love? I say answer hate with poise, and answer love with love.

§ Session 14.36

Confucius @MasterSays
Hardly anyone notices my talent.

Sly @Woodstock
And why do you think that is?

Confucius @MasterSays
It would be pointless to go around blaming people or circumstances. Suffice it to say that, where learning is concerned, I've worked my way up from the bottom. And if no one else, God will appreciate me for who I am.

§ Session 14.37

 Frank Underwood files a workplace grievance against **Louie** at the State Government. **Deep Throat** learns of the incident and comes ratting to **Confucius**.

Deep Throat @Messenger
That Underwood fellow is a piece of work. You just give the word, and I can have my boys make him disappear[20].

Confucius @MasterSays
No need for that. The fate of my movement is in the hands of God. If it's meant to be, nothing can stop our momentum. What could the likes of Underwood possibly do to trip us up?

§ Session 14.38

---

[20] Fellow minister Gōngbó Liáo speaks ill of Zǐlù (a.k.a. **Louie** @Walker) in front of Jì Sūn, head of the Jì clan, who employs them both. Lǔ minister Zǐfú Bójǐng relates the incident to Confucius and offers to "take care of" Gōngbó Liáo.

Confucius @MasterSays
The truly wise are able to detach themselves from this world; the next best thing is to tune out the chaos of your immediate surroundings. Failing that, try not be moved by fashions and fads, or, at the very least, don't be so easily swayed by words.

§ Session 14.39

Confucius @MasterSays
I know of seven such people.

§ Session 14.40

Louie spends the night at Los Angeles International Airport and is woken in the early hours by a security officer demanding to know where he is traveling from[21].

Louie @Walker
Ever heard of Master Confucius?

Airport Security @LAX
Oh yeah, that idiot who believes anything is possible.

§ Session 14.41

---

[21] Source text: " Zǐlù (a.k.a. **Louie** @Walker) spends the night at Stone Gate (one of the outer gates of the state of Lǔ) and is accosted by the gatekeeper as he awakes the next morning."

 **Confucius** is busking on the streets of New York when a particularly perceptive cab driver stops to listen[22].

Cabbie @YellowTaxi
The guy's got something on his mind.

The **Cabbie** then turns and comments:

 **Cabbie** @YellowTaxi
Now come on, if you can't it have your way, then it's time to let go. You gotta ride with the tide and go with the flow.

Confucius @MasterSays
That's one way to look at it. If only it were that easy.

§ Session 14.42

---

[22] Source text: "While traveling in the state of Wèi, Confucius was playing music on stone chimes when a porter stopped in front of his door to listen."

Ezra @Johnson
It is said that upon the death of Queen Victoria, the period of official mourning lasted a full year[23]. Is it true?

Confucius @MasterSays
It wasn't just Queen Victoria — extended periods of state mourning were common throughout history. When a monarch dies, the immediately family goes into mourning for a year, and day-to-day operations are taken over by a protocol officer.

§ Session 14.43

Confucius @MasterSays
When the guys at the top play by the rules, their followers willingly do their bidding.

§ Session 14.44

---

[23] Source text quotes the *Book of Documents*, Against Idleness: "When Shāng emperor Wǔ Dīng (1250-1192 BC) mourned the death of his father, he refrained from speech for a full three years."

Louie asks how to become somebody.

Confucius @MasterSays
Take yourself seriously.

Louie @Walker
That's it?

Confucius @MasterSays
Make other people take you seriously.

Louie @Walker
That's all there is to it?

Confucius @MasterSays
Make the world take you seriously. Now on that last point, I'm not sure even the Pope or the Dalai Lama have managed to pull it off[24].

§ Session 14.45

---

[24] Source text makes reference to the ancient sage kings Yáo and Shùn.

 Confucius sees **Estragon** squatting in a corner.

Confucius @MasterSays
Why, you pathetic loser! Unruly as a child, idle as an adult, and now an aging junkie living off welfare. You're better off dead[25].

 **Confucius** then raises his cane and whacks the vagabond on the leg.

§ Session 14.46

 A twelve-year-old prodigy serves as interpreter for the delegation from Moscow[26].

Interlocuter @Anonymous
Is the kid the real deal?

Confucius @MasterSays
Look at him, walking head to head with adults twice his age, so quick to take his seat among men of influence. The real deal? No way. He is a pure opportunist!

§ Session 14.47

---

[25] Source text: "Having shown no respect for your elders as a child, having contributed nothing to society as an adult, and now entering old age and not having the decency to die – why, you're nothing but a parasite!"

[26] Source text describes a crowd taken aback when the emissary from Confucius's home village of Què turns out to be an underage boy.

WARFARE

衛靈公

L'Empereur Napoléon inquires after theaters of war.

Confucius @MasterSays
You know, the Shakespearean theater I may know a thing or two about, but military theaters are not my thing[1].

Confucius packs up and leaves the very next day.

§ Session 15.01

 Confucius and entourage run out of provisions in Transylvania. Many in the party fall ill[2].

Louie @Walker
The Great Master in a state of despair. Who'd have thought I'd live to see this!

Confucius @MasterSays
Yeah, well, at least we're keeping our poise, whereas with some people, when things take a turn for the worse, anything goes.

§ Session 15.02

---

[1] King Líng of Wèi inquires after military strategy, to which Confucius replies, "I may know a thing or two about the ways of the kitchen, but was never schooled in the art of war."

[2] Confucius and entourage run out of provisions in the state of Chén — one of the many low points in the master's sojourns abroad.

Confucius @MasterSays
My dear Sly, do you really take me for some towering intellectual who possesses a vast store of knowledge acquired through tireless study?

Sly @Woodstock
Would I be wrong to do so?

Confucius @MasterSays
You are totally mistaken! What advice I dispense is drawn from a deceptively simple personal philosophy.

§ Session 15.03

Confucius @MasterSays
Louie, there are few left in this world who value sound moral judgment.

§ Session 15.04

Confucius @MasterSays
To wield influence without use of force: Mahatma Gandhi[3] comes to mind, who urged civil disobedience by simply setting an example for all.

§ Session 15.05

[3] Source text makes reference to the mythical emperor Shùn, who inspired awe by doing little more than sit ceremoniously in his throne facing south (NOTE: To "face south" is a metaphor for ruling over the masses. The expression is also used in Session 06.01, where **Roland** @Archer is said to possess qualities enabling him to "face south").

Confucius @MasterSays
Mean what you say and say it nicely; do what is promised and do it right. Keep to these principles and you'll be welcome even in the most outlandish of settings; fail to follow them and you'll be a pariah in your own back yard. Remember these words as if they're written on your forehead or printed on your bumper sticker[4].

Ezra has the words tattooed on his arm.

§ Session 15.06

---

[4] The importance of his advice on social acceptance is such that Confucius instructs Zǐzhāng (a.k.a. **Ezra** @Johnson) to "see these very words floating before your eyes" when standing in place, and to imagine them "carved into the interior of the carriage" when seated for travel. Zǐzhāng ends up writing the words on his sash.

Confucius @MasterSays
John Oliver is a firebrand who'll tell it like it is when the chemistry is right, and tell it like it is when the reception is hostile. Steve Jobs is a visionary who'll go all out when you share his vision, and simply walk away when his imagination isn't appreciated[5].

§ Session 15.07

Confucius @MasterSays
To speak when you shouldn't is to commit a faux pas; to hold back when you ought to speak is to squander an opportunity. Men of intellect don't commit faux pas, nor do they let opportunities slip by.

§ Session 15.08

Confucius @MasterSays
Better to die a martyr than to live in disgrace.

§ Session 15.09

---

[5] In the source text, Confucius praises Wèi minister Shǐ Yú for being "straight as an arrow" whether or not the political climate is favorable, in contrast to the style of fellow minister Qú Bóyù, who "steps up when needed and steps down when his services are no longer appreciated", which is different but equally admirable.

 **Sly** seeks advice on personal enrichment.

Confucius @MasterSays
To get the job done, you need the right tools. Wherever you go, rub shoulders with the powers that be and mingle with the brightest minds.

§ Session 15.10

Owen inquires after diplomatic decorum.

Confucius @MasterSays
Carry a Swiss timepiece, wear an Italian suit, and drive a German car. Only ever listen to classical music, and avoid the sounds of the ghetto. Ghetto sounds debase you, and ghetto types are nothing but trouble[6].

§ Session 15.11

Confucius @MasterSays
If you don't plan ahead, trouble won't be far behind.

§ Session 15.12

---

[6] Source text: "Observe the calendar of the Xià, ride in a chariot of the Shāng, and follow the fashions of the Zhōu. As for music, listen to the Sháo and the Wŭ, but avoid the sounds of the Zhèng, and beware of smooth talkers. Zhèng music borders on the obscene, whereas smooth talkers are always up to no good."

Confucius @MasterSays
Don't even get me started. I've yet to find someone who is turned on by good personality as much as he is turned on by good looks.

§ Session 15.13

Confucius @MasterSays
A usurper is Saul, who, knowing David is destined to be king, tries to rob him of his rightful place[7].

§ Session 15.14

Confucius @MasterSays
Be hard on yourself and kind to others — that's the way to win people over.

§ Session 15.15

Confucius @MasterSays
If you can't bring yourself to ask for help, I'm not sure there's anything I can do for you.

§ Session 15.16

---

[7] Source text: "This Zāng Wénzhòng (also see Session 05.18) is robbing a man of his job! He is fully aware of the talents of Liǔxià Huì, yet he squarely refuses to promote him."

Confucius @MasterSays
Out with the posse, talking trash all day, acting like a wisecrack — there's not much you can do for people like that.

§ Session 15.17

Confucius @MasterSays
Your typical stand-up guy is one who stands on principle and does things by the book. He'll stick to his word and keep a low profile. Now that's what you call a man!

§ Session 15.18

Confucius @MasterSays
Worry not about getting your fifteen minutes of fame, but about whether you have what it takes to make it big.

§ Session 15.19

Confucius @MasterSays
A shame to depart this life without leaving behind a legacy.

§ Session 15.20

Confucius @MasterSays
Great minds search within when things go wrong; lesser individuals look for people to blame.

§ Session 15.21

Confucius @MasterSays
A man of class is able to stand his ground without resorting to aggression, and can charm his friends while managing to be impartial.

§ Session 15.22

Confucius @MasterSays
Don't judge a man on his words alone; don't write someone off because of what he says.

§ Session 15.23

Sly @Woodstock
Is there a word of advice I can always count on to get me through the day?

Confucius @MasterSays
Reciprocity. Don't do to others what you don't want them to do to you.

§ Session 15.24

Confucius @MasterSays
When it comes to men of antiquity, there are those I praise and those I condemn. Those I praise receive my accolades because of deeds deserving, deeds epitomizing the glory of the Pax Romana[8].

§ Session 15.25

---

[8] Source text: "These men are the reason why the Three Dynasties of antiquity were able to keep to the straight path."

Confucius @MasterSays
Time was when ethnographers acknowledged gaps in our understanding of the world and looked to other cultures for answers. These days it's my way or the highway.

§ Session 15.26

Confucius @MasterSays
Fancy words obscure the truth. Sweat the small things, and you miss the big picture.

§ Session 15.27

Confucius @MasterSays
Just because he's a darling of the media, doesn't necessarily make him good; just because he's Public Enemy No. 1, doesn't necessarily make him bad.

§ Session 15.28

Confucius @MasterSays
It takes a visionary to preach the gospel. The gospel is not going to preach itself.

§ Session 15.29

Confucius @MasterSays
The biggest mistake of all is to not admit to your mistakes.

§ Session 15.30

Confucius @MasterSays
I've gone without food or sleep for an entire day looking for answers. Then it dawned on me, what's the point? It's easier just to ask somebody who knows.

§ Session 15.31

Confucius @MasterSays
Don't just get laid, get a life! Work and be rewarded for your labor. Get an education and double your earnings. It's not about the money, it's about finding your purpose in life.

§ Session 15.32

Confucius @MasterSays
If you have the brains to win office but not the heart to serve your people, don't expect to be in office for long. If you have the brains to win and the heart to serve, but don't look the part of a dignified statesman, don't expect be taken seriously. If you have the brains and the heart and also look the part, but don't play by the rules, don't expect to be shown any kindness.

§ Session 15.33

Confucius @MasterSays
Capable people may miss a detail here and there but they never fail to grasp the bigger picture. Dimwits get stuck on the minutiae and forget the greater purpose.

§ Session 15.34

Confucius @MasterSays
The desire to be civilized trumps the need for food and water. A shame people are willing to die for food and water, but not for a lesson in civility.

§ Session 15.35

Confucius @MasterSays
When you feel the call of duty, don't let anything stand in your way.

§ Session 15.36

Confucius @MasterSays
Be principled but not inflexible.

§ Session 15.37

Confucius @MasterSays
With government contracts, you deliver on your promises and *then* bill for your services.

§ Session 15.38

Confucius @MasterSays
With access to education, differences in background fade away[9].

§ Session 15.39

Confucius @MasterSays
When you don't see eye to eye, there's no point in working together.

§ Session 15.40

Confucius @MasterSays
Use words to get your point across — nothing more, nothing less.

§ Session 15.41

---

[9] One of Confucius's most quoted sayings, literally "have education, no categorization", which scholars over the ages have interpreted in numerous ways. The earliest surviving commentary is that of Hàn dynasty scholar Mǎ Róng 馬融 (79-166 A.D.), who writes "one is what one is because of education, regardless of prior background", in line with the conditional reading favored by the historical syntax of the Eastern Zhōu. Since the sixth century however, due in large part to the views of Liáng dynasty philologist Huáng Kǎn 皇侃, the most dominant reading of the passage is one that superimposes a first person "I" onto the sentence, giving "when I (Confucius) teach, I don't discriminate against students of different backgrounds". This is the interpretation found in most secondary school textbooks in East Asia. In other words, as a result of historical revisionism and folk etymology, a reading of the passage that most likely runs counter to Confucius's original intention has now been part of the Chinese psyche for over 1,500 years, and is deeply embedded in discourses on Chinese culture. The translation given in the present work follows Mǎ Róng's historical reading rather than Huáng Kǎn's subsequent interpretation, the latter of which forms the basis of most English language translations of the passage.

 **Confucius** receives **Stevie Wonder**[10], who, as he approaches the steps, is told by the master, "These are the steps," and as he nears his seat, is told by the master, "This is your seat." Once seated, the master proceeds to point out every individual in the audience.

Ezra @Johnson
So that is how you're supposed to speak to a blind person?

Confucius @MasterSays
That is indeed how you're supposed to speak to a blind person.

§ Session 15.42

---

[10] Source text: Confucius receives the blind musician Shī Miǎn (court musician of Lǔ) at his quarters.

STATECRAFT

季氏

Russia makes plans to annex the Ukrainian territory of Crimea. National security advisers **Randall** and **Louie** leak the news to **Confucius**, who is furious[1].

Confucius @MasterSays
How could you let this happen? Ukraine was the seat of Kievan Rus, whose leader Vladimir the Great converted Russia to Christianity. His son Yaroslav the Wise heralded a Golden Age in which Ukraine was the largest and most powerful state in Europe.

Randall @RandSays
It's not *my* idea. The president came up with the plan. Louie and I are dead set against it.

---

[1] Source text: The Jì clan makes plans to annex the neighboring territory of Zhuānyú. Jì family stewards Rǎn Yǒu (a.k.a. **Randall** @RandSays) and Zǐlù (a.k.a. **Louie** @Walker) inform Confucius.

Confucius @MasterSays
British Prime Minister Clement Attlee said it well, "If you're not up to the job, step down". Look at you two: the president is flirting with disaster and you just go along; the nation is teetering towards collapse and you're content to do nothing. What kind of security advisers are you? Just think, when a tiger escapes from the national zoo, do you blame the mayor or fault the zookeeper? When diamonds disappear from a safe deposit box, do you reprimand the owner or scrutinize bank security?

Randall @RandSays
But what with Ukraine moving closer to Europe and becoming a member of NATO, if Russia doesn't act now, it may never have the chance to do so again.

Confucius @MasterSays:
Funny how you're coming up with excuses for something you said you were dead set against. See, Russia's woes lie not in low currency reserves or a lack of sovereign territory; rather, it is social inequity and political instability that will ultimately bring it down. Your president ought to know that when wealth is distributed equitably, there is less resentment; when factions learn to get along, your support base grows; and when the general public feels secure, you're much more likely to stay in power. And by then, if neighboring states don't recognize you for the major player that you are, dazzle them with your technological advances and cultural achievements til their citizens come flocking to your borders. And when they do, welcome them with open arms. With the state that Russia is in now, thanks to you two idiots, foreign visitors shun the land, the economy is on the brink of collapse, and your president wants to launch a foreign incursion to divert attention. By then he will have bigger problems to worry about than the Crimea.

§ Session 16.01

Confucius @MasterSays
In a functioning democracy it is the president who enforces laws and treaties and serves as commander-in-chief of the armed forces. When central control weakens however the president becomes a mere figurehead beholden to the interests of governors who collect local taxes and command local militia. In federations where each state is a law unto itself, the union is unlikely to survive past its bicentennial. Even worse, where power rests with mayors and sheriffs, the country is lucky to make it past the century mark. And where local militias run amuck, the nation will likely fall in a matter of decades. For only when government is strong will policy not be overrun by local interests; only when government is strong will the people not take the law into their own hands.

§ Session 16.02

Confucius @MasterSays
It's been five generations since we've upheld the spirit of our Founding Fathers; for four generations the nation's been run by lobbyists and special interests. Picture Abraham Lincoln turning in his grave at what's become of his government of the people, by the people, and for the people[2].

§ Session 16.03

Confucius @MasterSays
There are friends who bring out the best in you, and there are friends who bring out the worst in you. Those who are knowledgeable, forthright, and reliable bring out the best in you. Those who are fawning, circumspect, and pretentious bring out the worst in you.

§ Session 16.04

---

[2] Source text: "It has been five generations since the royal house controlled its own finances; for four generations ministers wielded all political power — which is why the descendants of the House of Lǔ are in such a pitiable state."

Confucius @MasterSays
There are wholesome pastimes, and there are decadent pastimes. Wholesome pastimes include bonding with broad-minded friends, speaking out for charitable causes, and supporting music and the arts. Decadent pastimes include frivolous spending, aimless wandering, and non-stop partying.

§ Session 16.05

Confucius @MasterSays
When in the service of influential people, there are three no-no's: don't speak before you're told to speak, don't hold back when you're expected to speak, and don't speak without considering the consequences of your words.

§ Session 16.06

Confucius @MasterSays
You'll be battling three forces over the course of your life: in adolescence, as your metabolism surges, don't lightly bow to your libido; in the prime of your life, as your metabolism peaks, don't hungrily go for the kill; and in old age, as your metabolism slows, don't lazily succumb to greed.

§ Session 16.07

Confucius @MasterSays
Your average stand-up guy holds certain things in awe: he has a fear of God, shows respect for people in the know, and acknowledges the powers that be. The typical crackhead does not believe in God, pokes fun at people in the know, and are oblivious to the powers that be.

§ Session 16.08

Confucius @MasterSays
Fortunate are those who are born with the knowledge, less so those who have to learn, even less so those who struggle to learn, but the bottom of the heap is reserved for those who give up without a fight.

§ Session 16.09

Confucius @MasterSays
When looking, try to see the bigger picture, and when listening, make sure you thoroughly understand. Be approachable in demeanor and presentable in dress. Speak like you mean it and carry yourself professionally. When stumped, think about where to get answers, and in the heat of the moment, consider the consequences of your actions. And when presented with an opportunity to profit, ask yourself if it's too good to be true.

§ Session 16.10

Confucius @MasterSays
There are those who rush to do good and balk at the mere suggestion of impropriety. I've heard about people like that, and may even have met one or two. Then there are those who walk away from it all and live the pious life in quiet seclusion. I've heard about people like that, but have yet to come across one.

§ Session 16.11

Confucius @MasterSays
Emperor Nero presided over victorious legions, yet goes down in history as the madman who fiddled while the Eternal City burned. The apostle Paul was beheaded, and Peter put to death at the cross, yet they are celebrated as martyrs of the Christian faith[3]. They say "money can't buy you love". It isn't wealth or power that endears you to posterity, but the difference you make in the condition of your fellow man[4].

§ Session 16.12

---

[3] Source text: "King Jǐng of Qí was commander of chariots in the thousands, yet was not beloved of his own people, whereas Bó Yí and Shú Qí (also see Sessions 05.23 and 07.15) were left to starve at the foot of Shǒuyáng Hill, and are revered by the people to this day."

[4] Source text quotes the *Book of Songs*, Minor Odes, Fourth Decade, No. 4, "I Walk These Lonely Fields": "You leave me not for riches and wealth / but because you fell for someone else", albeit appropriating the lyrics to render a political reading.

Efron sidles up to **Gil**, son of Confucius.

Efron @Ziskind
So, do you get any special treatment?

Gil @Fishbourne
Umm…not really. Now there was one time when he stopped me as I was running across the courtyard and asked, "Have you read any Shakespeare, my son?" I said, "No," and he said, "How can you hope to master the English language if you don't read Shakespeare?" So I went and read *The Tragedies*. Then another time he stopped me and asked, "Have you read any Machiavelli, my son?" I said, "No," and he said "How can you hope to understand human nature if you don't read Machiavelli?" So I went and read *The Prince*. These are the two occasions that stick out in my mind[5].

Efron @Ziskind
Whoa, that's deep! So the lesson is, you have to read Shakespeare, you have to read Machiavelli, and you have to treat your son no differently from how you treat other people.

§ Session 16.13

---

[5] Instead of Shakespeare and Machiavelli, the source text quotes Confucius as encouraging his son to study the *Book of Songs* and the *Book of Rites*.

The wife of a British monarch is known to the sovereign as his Queen Consort or his Princess Consort, and is known to her subjects as Her Royal Majesty, Her Royal Highness, or Her Grace. Alternatively, people may choose to address her by her inherited title, such as the Duchess of Cornwall, or by her given name, such as Lady Diana, or simply as Madam[6].

§ Session 16.14

---

[6] Source text: "A sovereign addresses his wife as 'My Lady', whereas the wife refers to herself as 'your humble servant'. Subjects address the sovereign's wife as 'the Lady of Our Lord', though to citizens of other states she is referred to as 'our humble lesser sovereign'. Citizens of other states though refer to her as 'the Lady of the Lord'."

TEMPTATION

陽貨

 Joe McCarthy seeks to meet with Confucius but is turned down. He leaves behind a gold Rolex, which he figures the master, bound by the rules of polite society, would be forced to return. Confucius heads to the McCarthy residence with the knowledge that Senate is in session, only to run into the junior senator in the street[1].

Joe McCarthy @RedScare
Hey, we need to talk. Come on, do you really believe that by hiding out and refusing to serve your country, you'd be seen as some sort of hero?

Confucius @MasterSays
No.

Joe McCarthy @RedScare
And what with your lifelong ambition to serve all mankind, do you really think that by passing over this opportunity of a lifetime I am presenting to you, you are in the right state of mind?

Confucius @MasterSays
No.

---

[1] In the source text, Confucius turns down a meeting with Yáng Huò, steward of the Jì clan who ultimately leads a revolt against his masters. Yáng leaves behind a gift of a suckling pig, which Confucius, by custom, is forced to send back in person, thereby providing Yáng with an opportunity for engagement.

Joe McCarthy @RedScare
So what's it gonna be, my friend? Are you in, or what? My offer won't stand for much longer.

Confucius @MasterSays
Okay, okay. I'll come work for you.

§ Session 17.01

Confucius @MasterSays
Nature made us the same; nurture sets us apart.

§ Session 17.02

Confucius @MasterSays
Only geniuses and dimwits are adamant in their beliefs.

§ Session 17.03

 **Confucius** heads to the hillbilly town of Ozark, where **Yanni** is mayor. In the middle of the town square he sees **Yanni** playing Vivaldi's *Four Seasons* on his Stradivarius[2].

Confucius @MasterSays
Is there a point? Why bother to cast pearls before swine?

Yanni @Yannopolous
Back in the academy, we were taught that culture transforms. Exposure to the arts inspires lofty ideals in the ruling class, and encourages the laboring classes to identify with you.

Confucius @MasterSays
Of course you're right. Ignore my previous remark — that was my lame attempt at making a joke.

§ Session 17.04

---

[2] Source text relates how Confucius, on arriving at the town of Wǔchéng, presided over by his protégé Zǐyóu (a.k.a. **Yanni** @Yannopolous), hears a string ensemble and comments, "Why wield a hog splitter for the mere slaughter of chicken?"

 Il Duce **Benito Mussolini** invades Albania and calls **Confucius** to his aid. The master is tempted[3].

Louie @Walker
Have you nothing better to do than lick the boots of a fascist dictator?

Confucius @MasterSays
Look, the guy needs me. What can I say? Don't you see, I'm doing this for the sake of European unity.

§ Session 17.05

---

[3] Source text describes Confucius being summoned by the disaffected minister Gōngshān Fúrǎo, who, leveraging his control over the estate of Bì where he served, stages a rebellion against the Jì clan.

 **Ezra** asks about becoming a better person.

Confucius @MasterSays
There are five qualities you should seek to emulate if you are to become a man of the world.

Ezra @Johnson
And what might these five qualities be?

Confucius @MasterSays
The five qualities are humility, kindness, honesty, diligence, and generosity. Show humility to avoid shame and embarrassment, show kindness to win over hearts and minds, show honesty to earn the trust of your constituents, show diligence to achieve your goals in good time, and show generosity so strangers will gladly do your bidding.

§ Session 17.06

Louie @Walker:
You used to always say that "bad company corrupts good character". Do you not believe in that anymore? Why are you so eager to appease the Butcher of Bagdad?

Confucius @MasterSays
Yeah, yeah — so I did say that. But we're talking about me here, not you losers. My character is like a diamond so tough that nothing can ever break it; my conscience is of a clarity so pure that nothing can ever taint it. Besides, I'm no wallflower — I don't expect to be sitting on the sidelines all my life.

§ Session 17.07

Confucius @MasterSays
Louie, are you familiar with the six common failings of those with good intentions?

Louie @Walker
No, I am not.

---

[4] Source text describes Confucius being summoned by the disgraced Bì Xī, steward of the estate of Zhōngmóu, who plotted against his master Zhào Jiǎnzǐ, the most powerful minister in the state of Wèi.

Confucius @MasterSays
Sit. Let me tell you.

- Kindness gone unchecked makes you gullible;
- Cleverness gone unchecked makes you cynical;
- Loyalty gone unchecked makes you thuggish;
- Bluntness gone unchecked makes you tactless;
- Daring gone unchecked makes you reckless;
- Devotion gone unchecked makes you fanatical.

§ Session 17.08

Confucius @MasterSays
Guys, it confounds me why more people don't take a liking to rap music[5]. Rap, as a vehicle of expression, truly moves you; it heightens your senses; it raises awareness of social issues and provides a medium for people to vent their rage. From the ghettoes of the inner city to the highest corridors of power, people are ripe for rap artists to chronicle their struggles. If nothing else, it'll boost your street cred and bring you up to speed on the latest youth slang.

§ Session 17.09

---

[5] In the source text, Confucius propounds the merits of studying the *Book of Songs*.

Speaking to his son **Gil.**

Confucius @MasterSays
Have you ever listened to the Beatles
and the Rolling Stones?[6] You haven't
lived until you've listened to the Beatles
and the Rolling Stones.

§ Session 17.10

Confucius @MasterSays
The clamor of bells and drums — can
you really call that music? A smattering
of expensive clothes — can you really
call that taste?

§ Session 17.11

Confucius @MasterSays
A bully on the outside but a coward
within — I can think of few things more
despicable. Why, it's no better than a
pervert who peeps from a hole in the
wall!

§ Session 17.12

---

[6] Here Confucius singles out two collections from the *Book of Songs'* Airs
of the States: "South of Zhōu" and "South of Shào".

Confucius @MasterSays
Spineless appeasers are the scum of society.

§ Session 17.13

Confucius @MasterSays
Gossip-mongers are a menace to society.

§ Session 17.14

Confucius @MasterSays
Does an incompetent person deserve a job? You see, before he gets the job, he'll suspect they won't give it to him. Once he gets the job, he'll worry they're going to take it away from him. And once a man thinks they're out to steal his job, there's no telling what lengths he would go to.

§ Session 17.15

Confucius @MasterSays
Some qualities you find only in people of an earlier generation; these days they're much harder to come by:

- Hippies used to be free-spirited; these days they can get downright unruly;
- Recluses used to be withdrawn; these days they can be downright sociopathic;
- Dimwits used to be simple-minded; these days many are downright sneaky.

§ Session 17.16

Confucius @MasterSays
Guys who talk sweet and smile all the time are scum.

§ Session 17.17

Confucius @MasterSays
That preppy is out and punk is in, that metal bands draw bigger crowds than symphony orchestras, that angry tirades are the norm in the corridors of power — makes me wonder what the world is coming to[7].

§ Session 17.18

---

[7] Source text lists three of Confucius's pet peeves: the replacement of royal vermillion with the faddish color purple, the demise of classical music with the rise of Zhèng style crooning (also see Session 15.11), and the subversion of nations by lobbyists with the gift of the gab.

Confucius @MasterSays
I'm just going to shut up now.

Sly @Woodstock
If you keep quiet, how are we to know what to do?

Confucius @MasterSays
Look at God. Does God ever speak? And yet the seasons revolve in perfect rhythm while manifold creatures multiply and populate the earth. How does God get it done?

§ Session 17.19

When the **Shah of Iran**[8] requests an audience, **Confucius** feigns illness, ordering a servant to send him off. Yet just as the cleric is leaving, the master fiddles and sings at the top of his lungs, screaming loud and clear that he is anything but ill.

§ Session 17.20

---

[8] In the source text, Confucius refuses to see Rú Bēi, a native of Lǔ. Little is known about this character, with whom Confucius is so angry that he not only refuses an audience, but really rubs it in his face by letting the visitor know that he is available but just does not want to see him.

Butch @Self
In Victorian England, sons and daughters were expected to mourn the death of a parent for a full three years before returning to the workplace. Three years! Can you imagine? After three years, you'd lose your edge in the job market, and what skills you used to have would become obsolete. If you ask me, I'd say a year is time aplenty — a full rotation of the seasons ought to do the trick[9].

Confucius @MasterSays
Tell me you won't feel guilty wining, dining, and dressing to the nines a year into the death of your father or mother.

Butch @Self
I won't feel guilty.

Confucius @MasterSays
Well, if you say so. The average person would be in no mood to dress in fancy clothes, dine on extravagant foods, or dance to party mixes after a parent passes. But you're obviously not the average person. If it doesn't weigh on your conscience, then by all means, do what you have to do.

---

[9] In the source text, Zǎi Wǒ (a.k.a. **Butch** @Self) expresses disbelief at the three year mourning period that was standard in the day and suggests that it be changed to a year.

Butch leaves.

Confucius @MasterSays
What an ungrateful bastard! The average parent has to change three years' worth of diapers before a toddler can poop or pee on his own. Is it too much to ask a son to refrain from indulgence for three years as a token of his love for the parent?

§ Session 17.21

Confucius @MasterSays
Sitting around all day with nothing better to do — that's no way to lead a life. Why, even playing blackjack beats idling your time away.

§ Session 17.22

Louie @Walker
Is bravado overrated?

Confucius @MasterSays
Bravado needs to be tempered by good judgment. Guys who are brave but lack good judgment end up wreaking havoc; idiots with bravado but no sense of propriety end up behind bars.

§ Session 17.23

Sly @Woodstock
Does your mind ever fill with hatred for certain people?

Confucius @MasterSays
Tell me about it! When I see dimwits mocking greater minds, nitpickers dwelling on miniscule faults, daredevils reveling in unruly behavior, and fanatics driven by misguided faith, it really gets on my nerves. And yourself?

Sly @Woodstock
Oh, pseudo-science passing for scholarship, heresy touted as heroism, and slander disguised as social justice are what really gets me going.

§ Session 17.24

Confucius @MasterSays
Wimps and women are the hardest to please: befriend them and they walk all over you; hold back and they call you stand-offish.

§ Session 17.25

Confucius @MasterSays
If by age forty you're still a pain in the ass, you're a no hoper.

§ Session 17.26

SANCTUARY

微子

 **Paul** was beheaded, **Peter** put to death at the cross, and **John** banished to the ends of the earth[1].

 **Confucius** @MasterSays
Glory be to these martyrs of the Eternal City.

§ Session 18.01

 As unit manager at the Oswald Maximum Security Penitentiary, **Tim McManus** is repeatedly passed over for promotion[2]. He is asked, "Why don't you pack up and take your talents elsewhere?"

 **Tim McManus** @EmeraldCity
When you're outspoken as I am, you're going to be passed over for more tactful types no matter where you go; if you're cautious and devious, you don't have to go far to rise to the top.

§ Session 18.02

---

[1] Source text describes how the Shāng dynasty's most capable ministers ultimately desert the depraved Emperor Zhòu in his final days: Wēizǐ seeks refuge in a neighboring state; Jīzǐ is forced into enslavement, whereas Bǐgān takes his own life to make a point.

[2] The passage in the source text is centered on the fate of the talented Lǔ minister Liǔxià Huì, who, while serving as a corrections official, was removed from his post three times, ostensibly because of his propensity to call things as they are, refusing to bend to the will of the powers that be.

▶▶ **Confucius** interviews at Brownose University[3] and is addressed by the chair of the search committee.

Chair @Brownose
Your resume is extensive but your scholarship doesn't merit tenure. We can offer you a position as an adjunct.

▶▶ Days later he receives a letter explaining that the funding for the position did not come through.

Confucius vows never to set foot on their grounds again.

§ Session 18.03

▶▶ **Confucius** interviews at the Lothario Brothers, but loses out to the bosomy intern touting free concert tickets who goes away with the boss for the weekend[4].

Confucius vows never to do business with them again.

§ Session 18.04

---

[3] In discussing the rank at which to receive Confucius upon his visit to the Qí court, King Jǐng of Qí refuses to afford him the level of hospitality extended to the head of the powerful Jì clan, but proposes instead that he be placed somewhere between the leaders of the Jì and the Mèng clans, which Confucius considers humiliating.

[4] King Huán of Qí is presented with a gift of musicians and female dancers, in whose company he indulges himself for days, prompting Confucius to pack up and leave.

 An old fogey weaves through **Confucius's** motorcade, shouting to the people gathered in the street[5]:

 Enough is enough, it's time to wage war against the billionaires and corporate leaders!

---

[5] Source text describes an encounter between Confucius and Jiēyú the Madman of Chǔ, which is documented in multiple sources. According to the *Analects*, which casts Confucius in a more favorable light in this meeting of minds, Jiēyú deliberately shows up at Confucius's door and bursts into song before vanishing without a trace. The lyrics to the song, now known as the "Phoenix Song", is transcribed as thus in the *Analects*:

O precious phoenix incarnate,
Why grace a realm so degenerate?
The ghosts of the past we cannot slay,
But we'll live to fight another day—
Though you wonder if there is a point,
With overlords so keen to anoint
Another politician in a bubble
Eager to get us all in trouble!

He then bursts into song:

People killing, people dying,
Children hurt and you hear them crying,
Can you practice what you preach?
And would you turn the other cheek?

 **Confucius** steps out of his limo and wishes to speak to the man, but he is long gone[6].

§ Session 18.05

---

[6] A more detailed version of the lyrics is found in the *Zhuāngzǐ* (Inner Chapters, Human Realm), which lends a Taoist perspective to the encounter stripped of the positive tone found in the Confucian account:

O phoenix, why grace this decadent world?
What of the glorious past or the future bold?

Surrounded by angels you learn to give;
In a dog-eat-dog world you learn to live:
Why pass up on fun when it's free for the taking?
Why hesitate to dodge a disaster in the making?

Better yet why don't you stop pretending
That you're anything but condescending;
Step out of your high and mighty bubble
Before you get us all in trouble!

 **Confucius** and entourage wander off the beaten track to find **Slim Joe** and **Big Bubba** busy making hay in the pasture. **Louie** is sent to ask for directions.

Slim Joe @HammerNHoe
Who's the dude at the wheel?[7]

Louie @Walker
That would be my master Confucius.

Slim Joe @HammerNHoe
The sage Confucius?

Louie @Walker
That's right.

Slim Joe @HammerNHoe
Then he'll know how to get back onto the main road.

---

[7] Source text: "Who is the driver of the carriage?"

Louie turns to ask **Big Bubba**.

Big Bubba @HubbaHubba
And who might you be?

Louie @Walker
Call me **Louie**.

Big Bubba @HubbaHubba
So you're a follower of this Confucius
dude, I gather?

Louie @Walker
You got it!

Big Bubba @HubbaHubba
Let me tell you something, son.
Civilization is one big cesspool with no
one around to clean up the muck. Born
into this filth, better to join the team that
renounces the world than to follow some
dude who blames other men, don't you
think?

 With that, the pair resumes their haymaking.
Louie returns and relates the turn of events
to his party.

Confucius @MasterSays
Humans were never meant to live
among the birds and beasts. Do I have a
choice but to live among these men that
I loathe? If the world was in better
shape, do you think I'd want to be the
one going around mopping up the filth?

§ Session 18.06

▶▶ **Confucius** leads a field trip to Appalachia[8]. **Louie** falls behind and is separated from the group. He approaches a local hauling a sack full of farm tools.

Louie @Walker
Have you seen my professor?

Farmer @Hillbilly
Why, you proud, idle, privileged brat from the cities, how would I have any idea who your professor is?

▶▶ The rustic then duly empties his sack and begins to rake the leaves. **Louie** stands before him and bows. The farmer invites him to stay the night, cooks him a hearty meal, and introduces him to his two sons.

---

[8] Source text does not specify the location of the encounter.

 **Louie** leaves the next day and relates the turn of events to **Confucius**, who concludes that the farmer must be an eremite, and urges **Louie** to go seek him out. **Louie** returns to the house, but the farmer is long gone. He sighs.

Louie @Walker
Step out of the shadows, old man! Why let your abilities go to waste? If you can step in and help a hapless stranger, why not step up and help save the world? Can you live with yourself if you don't? Hiding out is a big mistake. Do the right thing and make yourself available. I know we don't live in the best of times, but what can you do?

§ Session 18.07

Confucius @MasterSays
We owe much to people living on the fringes, the likes of which include the Desert Fathers, Cuthbert of Lindisfarne, Hildegarde von Bingen, Martin Luther, Thomas More, Aung San Suu Kyi, and Nelson Mandela. These include visionaries who hold firm to their beliefs no matter the cost, such as Martin Luther and Thomas More, and those who are susceptible to compromise but unwavering in their faith, like Nelson Mandela and Aung San Suu Kyi. Others choose to withdraw from the world and freely speak their mind, like Cuthbert of Lindisfarne and Hildegarde von Bingen[9]. As for me, I'm not like them at all. I don't really insist this way or that; I'm more of a go-with-the-flow kind of guy.

§ Session 18.08

---

[9] Source text gives the following list of recluses: Bó Yí, Shú Qí, Yú Zhòng, Yí Yì, Zhū Zhāng, Liǔxià Huì, and Shào Lián. The martyred Shāng dynasty princes Bó Yí and Shú Qí have already been mentioned in Sessions 05.23, 07.15, and 16.12; accounts of the talented Lǔ minister Liǔxià Huì appear in Sessions 15.14 and 18.02. Little is known about the remaining characters on the list other than the fact that they were moral exemplars who chose to live life away from the maddening crowd.

Confucius @MasterSays
Looking back at the legendary Russian artists of the twentieth century, composers Igor Stravinsky and Sergei Rachmaninov both sought refuge in the United States from the two World Wars, dancers Rudolf Nureyev and Mikhail Baryshnikov defected respectively to France and Canada, cellist Mstislav Rostropovich lived in exile in Washington D.C., pianist Vladimir Horowitz rose to eminence in New York City, and violinist Jascha Heifetz eventually settled in sunny Southern California[10].

§ Session 18.09

---

[10] Source text gives the following list of musicians who, following the demise of court music during the reign of King Āi, left Confucius's native state of Lǔ to seek their fortunes elsewhere: principle conductor Maestro Zhì (who left for the state of Qí), second conductor Maestro Gān (who left for the state of Chǔ), third conductor Maestro Liáo (who left for the state of Cài), fourth conductor Maestro Quē (who left for the state of Qín), tympanist Fāng Shú (who settled on the banks of the Yellow River), drummer Wǔ (who moved to the shores of the River Hàn), and percussionist-cum-junior concertmaster Yáng (who moved to the seaside).

To the **Pharaoh of Egypt**.

Joseph @DreamProphet
Don't desert those closest to you; don't make them feel neglected. Unless they're really out of line, don't give up on them. Remember, nobody's perfect.

§ Session 18.10

Confucius @MasterSays
Behold! The founding fathers of the United States of America: George Washington, John Adams, Thomas Jefferson, James Madison, Alexander Hamilton, James Monroe, and Benjamin Franklin[11].

§ Session 18.11

---

[11] Source text attributes the might of the Zhōu to its recruitment of loyalists of the Shāng, whose dynasty it had replaced. Many of these individuals had initially gone into hiding, and are thus categorized as recluses by the Confucian school. Few details remain of the lives of these converts, whose ranks include Bó Dá, Bó Kuò, Zhòng Tū, Zhòng Hū, Shú Yè, Shú Xià, Jì Suí, and Jì Guā. Note the symmetry in the birth rank of the listed individuals, which include two first-borns (prefix Bó), two second-borns (prefix Zhòng), two third-borns (prefix Shú), and two fourth-borns (prefix Jì), due to which Hàn dynasty commentator Bāo Xián (7-65 A.D.) believes the list to consist of four sets of identical twins.

CHIVALRY

子張

Ezra @Johnson
If you're willing to risk your life in the face of danger and forgo personal gain in the name of honor, if you're pious in prayer and solemn in mourning, then yeah, I guess you could call yourself a decent human being.

§ Session 19.01

Ezra @Johnson
People with questionable morals and wavering faith are expendable.

§ Session 19.02

 A follower of **Auguste** approaches **Ezra** for advice on friendship.

Ezra @Johnson
What did Auguste tell you?

Interlocuter @Anonymous
He said to bond with those who are worth your while and not waste time on the rest.

Ezra @Johnson
I see things somewhat differently, for aren't we supposed to honor the wise and rally the meek, promote the strong and shelter the weak? If wisdom and strength are within me, wouldn't I want to save every lost soul on earth? And if in these areas I am lacking, I'd be lucky to have anyone befriend me, let alone give me the chance to unfriend them.

§ Session 19.03

Auguste @LeMerchant
Even the most menial pursuits advance our understanding of the world, but don't miss the forest for the trees.

§ Session 19.04

Auguste @LeMerchant
To learn something new with each passing day and not ignore the lesson as the months go by is to be a champion of lifelong learning.

§ Session19.05

Auguste @LeMerchant
When you read broadly and exhibit focus, when you probe deeply and ask pertinent questions, you are a humanist par excellence.

§ Session19.06

Auguste @LeMerchant
Skilled workers enter apprenticeships to learn the tools of their trade; great minds go to university to acquire the ways of the world.

§ Session 19.07

Auguste @LeMerchant
Only a wuss would make a mistake and try to cover it up.

§ Session 19.08

Auguste @LeMerchant
Righteous folk strike you as intimidating, though once you get to know them they're remarkably accommodating, except on matters of principle, where they're dogged and uncompromising.

§ Session 19.09

Auguste @LeMerchant
Earn the respect of your employees before putting them to work — if not they'll think you're exploiting them; earn the trust of your supervisor before pointing out his faults — if not he'll think you're mocking him.

§ Session 19.10

Auguste @LeMerchant
Turn a blind eye to the little things, but stand your ground on matters of principle.

§ Session 19.11

Yanni @Yannopolous
By getting his naive young interns to do his laundry and housekeeping as well as staff his front desk and take his calls, don't you think Auguste is profiting off their labor and providing very little guidance in return?

Auguste @LeMerchant
How dare you, Yanni! When it comes to life's lessons, who's to say what's to come first and what's to come later? It's not like growing herbs, where you have a Farmer's Almanac to tell you what is in season. If it was as easy as that, where we could all go by the book and churn out saints by the dozen, where's the challenge in educating the next generation?

§ Session 19.12

Auguste @LeMerchant
Most academics could use some real world experience; most real world professionals would do well to go back to school.

§ Session 19.13

Yanni @Yannopolous
At a funeral, don't be afraid to let it all out.

§ Session 19.14

Yanni @Yannopolous
My friend Ezra is better than most people, but I wouldn't call him perfect.

§ Session 19.15

Jonathan @JonoSays
As impressive as Ezra may look, he isn't someone you would want take home to meet your parents.

§ Session 19.16

Jonathan @JonoSays
I was told by the master that if there ever is sorrow that comes straight from the heart, it is when a beloved parent passes on.

§ Session 19.17

Jonathan @JonoSays
The master once told me that the remarkable thing about King Solomon is his honoring of the legacy of his father, preserving continuity in government and personnel. Solomon's other exploits were impressive too, but his honoring of his father's legacy is a story for the ages[1].

§ Session 19.18

---

[1] Source text: "The master once commented that while other aspects of Mèng Zhuāngzǐ's filial behavior can be replicated, it is his honoring of his father's legacy, preserving continuity in government and personnel, that is truly remarkable."

 **Cornelius** is nominated by the president to become the next Supreme Court justice, and seeks advice from **Jonathan** about his appointment[2].

Jonathan @JonoSays
What with the moral vacuum at the top, the people are disillusioned and are lashing out. If you find evidence of their wrongdoing, be lenient and take into account the political circumstances.

§ Session 19.19

Sly @Woodstock
You know, Brutus probably wasn't as bad as people make him out to be[3]. So the moral is, be good, or else the evils of the world will be added to your rap sheet.

§ Session19.20

---

[2] Yáng Fū, newly appointed to the office of judge by the Mèng clan, seeks advice from his master Zēngzǐ (a.k.a. **Jonathan** @JonoSays) on his new position.

[3] Source text: "The depraved last emperor Zhòu of the Shāng dynasty (also see Session 18.01) probably wasn't as bad as people make him out to be."

Sly @Woodstock
Liken your mistakes to a solar eclipse: put them out there for everyone to see — because when it is over, when the sky returns to its natural brightness, the multitudes look up in wonder.

§ Session 19.21

Gaspard Matin @LeComte
This professor of yours, Confucius — what are his academic credentials?

Sly @Woodstock
You know, the traditions of Greece and Rome are not all lost — they are to be found among the people[4]. The high arts are preserved among society's elite; the low culture kept alive by the working classes. It is through exposure to these living arts that my master acquired his knowledge. So formal credentials, no, but there is no denying his classical upbringing.

§ Session19.22

---

[4] Source text: "The spirit of our founding emperors Wén and Wǔ is not lost to us — it is to be found among the common people."

 **Francesco Sforza** swears before the pope that **Sly** is far more qualified than **Confucius**. **Sly** learns of the incident via **Deep Throat**.

Sly @Woodstock
Let me put it this way. Me, I'm your typical suburban house with a white picket fence — the man in the street can easily peer over the fence and judge the worth of my property. Confucius, on the other hand, is like a million-dollar mansion surrounded by ten-foot walls, the riches and splendors of which are not visible to your average Joe. If you've never been invited in, you'll have no idea how luxurious it is. Given Francesco Sforza's level of sophistication, don't you think it is only natural he'd prefer my humble talents over the genius of the master?

§ Session 19.23

 **Francesco Sforza** goes around spreading falsehoods about **Confucius**.

Sly @Woodstock
Save your breath. The man cannot be brought down. You see, while other gurus are like hilltops within your reach, Confucius is up there with the sun and the moon. You want to bring down the sun and the moon? Good luck. I doubt the sun and the moon are going to be knocked from their orbits anytime soon; rather, it is your sanity that appears to be veering off course.

§ Session 19.24

Efron @Ziskind
You are every bit the perfect gentleman.
I cannot imagine your master Confucius
being any more charming than you are.

Sly @Woodstock
Surely you have misspoken, which you
should take care not to do again, for
posterity will judge you by your words.
But my point is, to compare me with the
master is preposterous, for he is up
there with the stars and the moon, the
dizzying heights of which no human can
ever hope to reach. As minister of a
state, his authority is such that if he says
jump we'll ask how high; if he says bark
we'll ask how loud — we are completely
at his beck and call. We marvel at his
many achievements in life, and, when
the time comes, will surely mourn the
tragedy of his passing. In every way he
looms larger than life — how can I even
dream of being his equal?

§ Session 19.25

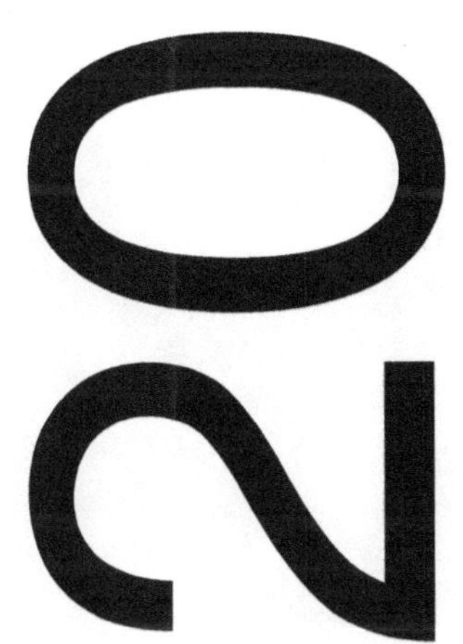

MANDATE

堯日

Jesus @Nazareth to **Joseph** @Arimathea
I trust you, Joseph, to be keeper of this Grail[1], this eternal fountain of joy, fulfillment, and admiration in both this world and the next. Be fair and use its powers for good, for should mankind suffer for your ineptness, the Lord will stand with you no more.

 The admonition is handed down faithfully to **Galahad** and **Perceval**.

§ Session 20.01

Fisher King @CastleOfSouls
God be my witness, upon the blood of this sacrificial bull, I, Pelles, pledge fealty to the Grail[2] and swear to bring down its enemies, be they peasants or princes, strangers or kinsfolk. Should my subjects incur the wrath of God, let them off lightly and lay blame on their king; should I their king be found inept, punish me and me alone -- do not lay waste to the livelihoods of my people.

§ Session 20.02

---

[1] Source text quotes Emperor Yáo's admonitions to his chosen successor Shùn: "Heed my words, O wise Shùn, for the fate of the world lies in your hands. Adjudicate in all fairness, for if your people languish in misery, the mandate of heaven will be yours no longer."

[2] Source text: "I, your most humble servant Lǚ, dare offer for sacrifice this black bull and pledge to you, most noble and gracious of lords, that, under my rule, no crime shall go unpunished, even if the offenders be royalty or high officials, for no deed or action escapes your omniscience..."

 In the far reaches of Araby lies the terrestrial paradise of **Prester John**, illustrious king and beloved son of Christ, whose vast multitude of loyal subjects populate his sumptuous kingdom[3].

Prester John @Nestorian
Though I am not without sons and brothers, is it not better to engage the services of those more able? Should my subjects err in the eyes of the Lord, blame me and me alone.

§ Session 20.03

Confucius @MasterSays
The sage kings of old have taught us that a world class state is built upon human capital, infrastructure, and the rule of law. To win over hearts and minds, the ruler must further take in the undocumented, employ the jobless and house the homeless. Give them food and shelter; let them practice their faith and mourn their dead.

§ Session 20.04

---

[3] Source text: "Through the contributions of vassals from the far reaches of the Zhōu empire, the lives of our good citizens have been enriched..."

Confucius @MasterSays
Tolerance precludes misgivings and faith breeds trust; fairhandedness dispels resentment and dedication delivers results.

§ Session 20.05

Ezra @Johnson
How does one become an effective leader?

Confucius @MasterSays
You'll want to possess the five essential qualities of the successful leader and avoid the four common pitfalls.

Ezra @Johnson
What are the five essential qualities?

Confucius @MasterSays
You'll want to be gracious but not extravagant, demanding though not harsh, ambitious without succumbing to greed, self-assured without appearing arrogant, and inspire awe without instilling fear in the hearts of your people.

Ezra @Johnson
What do you mean by "gracious but not extravagant"?

Confucius @MasterSays
You see, when you provide to your people the bare essentials, you are gracious without being extravagant; when you ask of your people what is within their reach, you are demanding but not unreasonable; when you chase after lofty aspirations, you look to be ambitious but not greedy; when you serve people regardless of status or station, you show poise without appearing aloof; and when you dress respectably and project assurance in your demeanor, you inspire awe but do not strike fear in those who look up to you.

Ezra @Johnson
And what about the four common pitfalls?

Confucius @MasterSays
Never mete out punishment without due process; never ask beyond what is humanly possible; never change the rules late in the game, and never skimp on rewards to those who deliver.

§ Session 20.06

Confucius @MasterSays
Without a sense of purpose, you'll never reach your full potential; without regard for protocol, you'll never find your place in the world; without a way with words, you'll never share camaraderie with your fellow man.

§ Session 20.07

2

INQUIRY
(fragments)

問
玉

Sly @Woodstock
Why is jade so expensive and marble so cheap? Is it because marble is plentiful and jade is not?[1]

Confucius @MasterSays
It isn't to do with marble being common, but to do with the fact that jade possesses qualities sought after by the most discerning individuals: with a luster soft and silky smooth, it resembles one who is gentle; with a chime that reverberates far and wide, it resembles one who is wise; with a girdle that would sooner break than bend, it resembles one who is firm; with an edge that is keen but does not bite, it resembles one who is sharp; with an exterior that lays bare the blemishes within, it resembles one who is frank. Hence the popular lyric:

---

[1] Translated from the fragment 之方也思理自外可以知 from Slip No. 73EJH1:58 unearthed at the Western Hàn dynasty fortification of Jiānshuǐ Jīnguān 肩水金關 (121-102 B.C.) preserved in the Gobi Desert, located in present-day Gānsù province, whose contents were first made public in 2016. Identical language appears under the entry for "jade" 玉 in the Hàn dynasty dictionary *Shuōwén Jiězì* (100-121 A.D.), the full text of which is used here to reconstruct the original passage, believed to be quoted from the Qí recension of the Confucian *Analects*. Similar discourses appear in the Proper Conduct 法行 chapter of the *Xúnzǐ*, the Diplomatic Mission 聘義 chapter of the *Book of Rites*, and the Inquiry into Jade 問玉 chapter of the *Family Sayings of Confucius*.

For the one I love I prayed,
Whose heart is pure as jade[2].

§ Session 21.01

Confucius @MasterSays
Love thyself — 'tis the key to fulfillment.
Know thyself — 'tis the key to wisdom[3].

§ Session 21.02

---

[2] From the *Book of Songs*, Airs of Qín #3, "Little Chariot".

[3] From Slip No. 73EJT31:139 unearthed at the Western Hàn fortification of Jiānshuǐ Jīnguān 肩水金關 (121-102 B.C.).

GNOSIS
(fragments)

知
道

 When **Confucius** first saw the light, so moved was he that for days on end he wanted nothing than to bask in the warmth of its balmy glow.

 **Confucius** @MasterSays
So magnificent is this universal order that one cannot but succumb to its stunning beauty[1].

§ Session 22.01

---

[1] Translated from the fragment 孔子智道之易也易易云者三日子曰此道之美也莫之御也, first made public in 2016, from the Western Han dynasty tomb of Liú Hè 劉賀 (92-69 B.C.), Marquis of Haihun, located in present-day Jiāngxī province. A similar fragment 孔子知道之易也易々云者三日子曰此道之美也 appears as Slip No. 73EJT22:6 in the texts unearthed at Jiānshuǐ Jīnguān 肩水金關 (121-102 B.C.) in the Gobi desert. The fragment is believed by many to form the opening lines of the Zhīdào 知道 chapter of the long lost Qí recension of the Confucian *Analects*. Similar discourses appear in the Festive Drinking 鄉飲酒義 chapter of the *Book of Rites*, the Discourse on Music 樂論 in the *Xúnzǐ*, and the Yán Huí 顏回 chapter of the *Family Sayings of Confucius*. Here we interpret the key character 易 as a pre-Qín orthographic variant of 陽 ("sunny"; "shining"; "radiant") rather than as a corruption of the character 易 ("replace"; "change"; "alternate"; "simple").

Sly @Woodstock
One tribe,
One time,
One planet,
One race.

When the rainbow nations gather as one, the revolution will have begun. Until then we wait, living in fear, as innocents are persecuted by the state[2].

We didn't start the fire;
It was always burning
Since the world's been turning[3].

Confucius @MasterSays
We didn't start the fire,
But when we are gone,
Will it still burn on and on?[4]

§ Session 22.02

---

[2] From Slip No. 73EJC:608 unearthed at the Western Hàn fortification of Jiānshuǐ Jīnguān 肩水金關 (121-102 B.C.). Source text gives the lines 九變復貫 / 知言之纂, i.e., "When nine tribes come together as one / The jubilee cycle will be refreshed", purportedly from the unabridged *Book of Songs*, a variant of which is found in the Annals of Emperor Wu in the *Book of Hàn* (111).

[3] From the *Book of Songs*, Minor Odes, Fourth Decade #8, "First Month": "Living anxiously / Fearing oppression by the state".

[4] From the *Book of Songs*, Airs of Chen #3, "Roof": "A roof over your head / A place to catch your breath".

Cast of Characters

Confucius and Family

Zhòng Ní 仲尼 [known as 孔子]
(born **Kǒng Qiū** 孔丘)

RENDERED AS
Confucius @MasterSays

Bó Yú 伯魚 [son of Confucius]
(born **Kǒng Lǐ** 孔鯉)

RENDERED AS
Gil @Fishbourne

Gōngyě Cháng 公冶長
[son-in-law]

RENDERED AS
Jailbird John @LongJohn

Nán Róng 南容 [niece's husband]
(born **Nángōng Kuò** 南宮括)

RENDERED AS
Dixie Chet @Antebellum

Yán Yuān 顏淵
(born **Yán Huí** 顏回)

RENDERED AS
Owen @Yentl

Zǐ Qiān 子騫
(born **Mǐn Sǔn** 閔損)

RENDERED AS
Mason @Withers

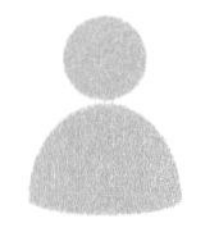

Bó Niú 伯牛
(born **Rǎn Gēng** 冉耕)

RENDERED AS
Rhett @Wrangler

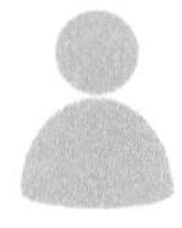

Zhòng Gōng 仲弓
(born **Rǎn Yōng** 冉雍)

RENDERED AS
Roland @Archer

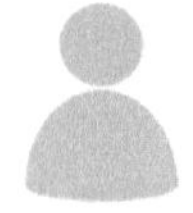

Rǎn Yǒu 冉有 [known as 冉子]
(born **Rǎn Qiú** 冉求)

RENDERED AS
Randall @RandSays

Zǐ Lù 子路
(born **Zhòng Yóu** 仲由)

RENDERED AS
Louie @Walker

Zǎi Wǒ 宰我
(born **Zǎi Yú** 宰予)

RENDERED AS
Butch @Self

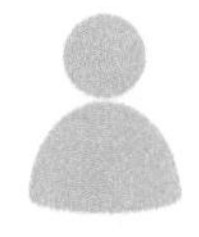

Zǐ Yú 子輿 [known as 曾子]
(born **Zēng Shēn** 曾參)

RENDERED AS
Jonathan @JonoSays

Zēng Xī 曾皙
(born **Zēng Diǎn** 曾點)

RENDERED AS
Jonah @White

Qīdiāo Kāi 漆彫開
(born **Qīdiāo Qǐ** 漆彫啟)

RENDERED AS
Chad @Carver

Yǒu Ruò 有若
[known as 有子]

RENDERED AS
Hubert @EubieSays

Zǐ Huá 子華
(born **Gōngxī Chì** 公西赤)

RENDERED AS
Florian @Westwood

Zǐ Gòng 子貢
(born **Duānmù Sì** 端木賜)

RENDERED AS
Sly @Woodstock

Zǐ Xià 子夏
(born **Bǔ Shāng** 卜商)

RENDERED AS
Auguste @LeMerchant

Qín Láo 琴牢

RENDERED AS
Cameron @Locke

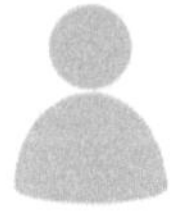

Zǐ Gāo 子羔
(born **Gāo Chái** 高柴)

RENDERED AS
Garth @Lamb

Fán Chí 樊遲
(born **Fán Xū** 樊須)

RENDERED AS
Francis @Waite

Yuán Sī 原思
(born **Yuán Xiàn** 原憲)

RENDERED AS
Shane @McEwan

Sīmǎ Niú 司馬牛
(born **Sīmǎ Gēng** 司馬耕)

RENDERED AS
Seymour @McKnight

Disciples (from the state of Chén)

Zǐ Zhāng 子張
(born **Zhuānsūn Shī** 顓孫師)

RENDERED AS
Ezra @Johnson

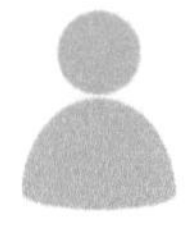

Wūmǎ Qí 巫馬旗
(born **Wūmǎ Shī** 巫馬施)

RENDERED AS
Omar @Chayil

Zǐ Qín 子禽
(born **Chén Kàng** 陳亢)

RENDERED AS
Efron @Ziskind

Disciples (from the state of Wú)

Zǐ Yóu 子游
(born **Yán Yǎn** 言偃)

RENDERED AS
Yanni @Yannopolous

Duke of Zhōu 周公

RENDERED AS
Joseph @DreamProphet

King Jǐng of Qí 齊景公

RENDERED AS
Louis XIV @theSunKing

King Líng of Wèi 衛靈公

RENDERED AS
L'Empereur Napoléon @Bonaparte

King Dìng of Lǔ 魯定公

RENDERED AS
King Frederick @SleepyHead

King Āi of Lǔ 魯哀公

RENDERED AS
King Maximilian @LastKnight

King Āi of Lǔ 魯哀公 (Session §14.22)

RENDERED AS
Obama @44thPresident

Jì Kāngzǐ 季康子

RENDERED AS
Cosimo de Medici @ilGrande

Jì Zǐrán 季子然

RENDERED AS
Lorenzo de Medici @ilMagnifico

Royals (from the House of Mèng)

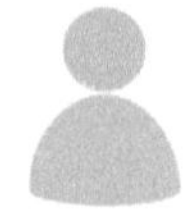

Mèng Yìzǐ 孟懿子

RENDERED AS
Cesare de Borgia @DucaValentino

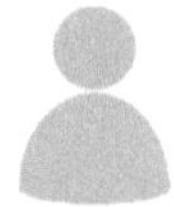

Mèng Wǔbó 孟武伯

RENDERED AS
Rodrigo de Borgia @AlexanderVI

Mèng Jìngzǐ 孟敬子

RENDERED AS
Alfonso de Borgia @CalixtusIII

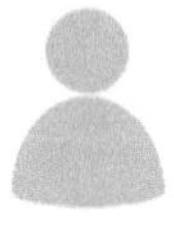

Shúsūn Wǔshú 叔孫武叔

RENDERED AS
Francesco Sforza @ilDuchetto

Lín Fàng 林放

RENDERED AS
Pierre Larousse @Encyclopedie

Zǐsāng Bózǐ 子桑伯子

RENDERED AS
Diogenes @Sinope

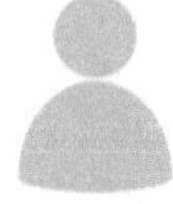

Wēishēng Mǔ 微生畝

RENDERED AS
Peewee @Misanthrope

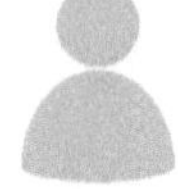

Zǐfú Jǐngbó 子服景伯

RENDERED AS
Deep Throat @Messenger

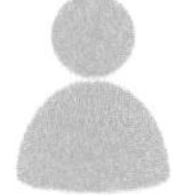

Yuán Ráng 原壤

RENDERED AS
Estragon @Gogo

Contemporaries (from the state of Lǔ)

Shī Miǎn 師冕

RENDERED AS
Stevie Wonder @LittleStevie

Yáng Huò 陽貨

RENDERED AS
Joe McCarthy @RedScare

Yáng Fū 陽膚

RENDERED AS
Cornelius @Gosefordsich

Contemporaries (from the state of Chǔ)

Yè Gōng 葉公

RENDERED AS
Ole McCoy @Appalachia

Cháng Jǔ 長沮

RENDERED AS
Slim Joe @HammerNHoe

Jié Nì 桀溺

RENDERED AS
Big Bubba @HubbaHubba

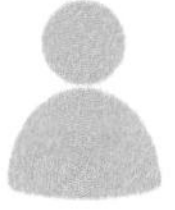

Wángsūn Jiǎ 王孫賈

RENDERED AS
Joachim Murat @GrandeArmée

Jí Zǐchéng 棘子成

RENDERED AS
Guy Duchamps@Ministre

Gōngmíng Jiǎ 公明賈

RENDERED AS
Henry Halleck @OldBrains

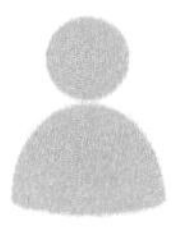

Gōngsūn Cháo 公孫朝

RENDERED AS
Gaspard Matin @LeComte

Chén Sībài 陳司敗

RENDERED AS
Judge Judy @JusticeServed

Yáo 堯 (Session §20.01)

RENDERED AS
Jesus @Nazareth

Shùn 舜 (Session §20.01)

RENDERED AS
Joseph @Arimathea

Shùn 舜 (Session §20.02)

RENDERED AS
Fisher King @CastleOfSouls

Liǔxià Huì 柳下惠

RENDERED AS
Tim McManus @EmeraldCity